Language

Learn How to Persuade People Using Mind Control, Nlp Manipulation, Cbt, Persuasion Methods and Subliminal Hypnosis

(With Secret Techniques Against Deception and Brainwashing)

Paul Morris

Published by Kevin Dennis

Paul Morris

All Rights Reserved

Body Language: Learn How to Persuade People Using Mind Control, Nlp Manipulation, Cbt, Persuasion Methods and Subliminal Hypnosis (With Secret Techniques Against Deception and Brainwashing)

ISBN 978-1-989965-17-7

All rights reserved. No part of this guide may be reproduced in any form without permission in writing from the publisher except in the case of brief quotations embodied in critical articles or reviews.

Legal & Disclaimer

The information contained in this book is not designed to replace or take the place of any form of medicine or professional medical advice. The information in this book has been provided for educational and entertainment purposes only.

The information contained in this book has been compiled from sources deemed reliable, and it is accurate to the best of the Author's knowledge; however, the Author cannot guarantee its accuracy and validity and cannot be held liable for any errors or omissions. Changes are periodically made to this book. You must consult your doctor or get professional medical advice before using any of the suggested remedies, techniques, or information in this book.

Upon using the information contained in this book, you agree to hold harmless the Author from and against any damages, costs, and expenses, including any legal fees potentially resulting from the application of any of the information provided by this guide. This disclaimer applies to any damages or injury caused by the use and application, whether directly or indirectly, of any advice or information presented, whether for breach of contract, tort, negligence, personal injury, criminal intent, or under any other cause of action.

You agree to accept all risks of using the information presented inside this book. You need to consult a professional medical practitioner in order to ensure you are both able and healthy enough to participate in this program.

TABLE OF CONTENTS

INTRODUCTION 1

CHAPTER 1: WHY SHOULD WE LEARN HOW TO READ PEOPLE BETTER? 5

CHAPTER 2: DIVING INTO THE HUMAN MIND 6

CHAPTER 3: THE IMPORTANCE OF SELF-AWARENESS 13

CHAPTER 4: THE ALPHA MALE: HOW TO SPOT ONE 21

CHAPTER 5: THE BASICS OF BODY LANGUAGE 33

CHAPTER 6: WHAT DOES BODY LANGUAGE ENTAIL? 38

CHAPTER 7: INTRODUCTION TO COMMUNICATION 46

CHAPTER 8: COMMUNICATING WITH BODY LANGUAGE . 50

CHAPTER 9: TYPES OF BODY LANGUAGE 54

CHAPTER 10: READING BETWEEN THE LINES 58

CHAPTER 11: THE FINALE 66

CHAPTER 12: THE ART OF SUBTLE PEOPLE ANALYSIS 71

CHAPTER 13: READING PEOPLE THROUGH THEIR WORDS 79

CHAPTER 14: USING BODY LANGUAGE EFFECTIVELY 86

CHAPTER 15: THE HISTORY AND BACKGROUND 91

CHAPTER 16: NON-VERBAL COMMUNICATION 98

CHAPTER 17: PRACTICE MAKES PERFECT 112

CHAPTER 18: WELL ARMED 119

CHAPTER 19: BODY LANGUAGE 122

CHAPTER 20: THE ART OF FLIRTING 140

CHAPTER 21: THE FOUR PERSONALITY TYPES 159

CHAPTER 22: WHAT IS EMOTIONAL INTELLIGENCE? 169

CHAPTER 23: SIGNIFICANCE OF YOUR VERBAL AND NON-VERBAL CUES 176

CHAPTER 24: HOW TO DELIVER A SPEECH AND CONNECT TO THE AUDIENCE 183

CHAPTER 25: TONES OF VOICE 190

CHAPTER 26: INTROVERTS VS. EXTROVERTS 195

CONCLUSION 203

Introduction

How to influence people in life and love.

We live in a world where our lives depend on one another; nobody or no one can live in isolation we all need one another in our individual lives. More often than not we tend to take people in our lives for granted that we often neglect some smaller details of people that surround us be it families, friends, neighbors and so on.

Everybody needs a relationship starting from the family circle, nobody can't be said to be exempted from a relationship because influence and love start from having a relationship with people. It means there's something bringing or binding people together. Be it, family, workplace, the neighbor next door or in a team.

Day in and day out, we spend most of our time thinking about ourselves. But if we stop thinking about ourselves for a bit and start thinking about other people's strengths, we wouldn't have to resort to cheap flattery and we could offer honest sincere appreciation.

With words of true appreciation, we have the power to completely change another person's perception of themselves, improve their motivation, and be a driving force behind their success. When you structured your thinking like that - when we have nothing to lose and only positive outcomes to gain - why wouldn't we offer genuine appreciation more often?

This principle is absolutely key in influencing others.

To convince someone to do something, we have to frame it in terms of what motivates them. And in order to do that, we have to be able to see things from their point of view as well as our own.

Most salespeople spend a lifetime selling without seeing things from the customer's angle, wondering why they're not successful as they completely ignore the customer's needs.

If we can put aside our own thoughts, opinions, and wants, and truly see things from another person's perspective, we will be able to convince them that it is in their best interest to do whatever it is we're after.

"The world is full of people who are grabbing and self-seeking. So the rare individual who unselfishly tries to serve others has an enormous advantage. He has little competition."

What do the world's best leaders know that the rest of us don't? How do you become an influencer without feeling like a sleazy salesman? How do you connect with important people and get your reputation to spread?

And for years, I didn't understand it myself. It's this: Why can't I get more influence?

The answer may surprise you.

The Secret To Gaining Influence

Some people don't want you to know this. It's a secret long held by the social elite, what builds dynasties and topples kingdoms. It's the explanation for how even the humblest of beginnings can lead to the strongest successes.

This is important for you to hear, and it could be the answer to getting your book published or launching a successful business. It might even mean landing that connection that changes everything.

We doubt ourselves, thinking we don't have what it takes. We give in to fear and sabotage ourselves before we even begin. We are our own worst enemy.

Below are few methods that will help you to influence more people in life and love:

Show Genuine Interest In Someone Else

Remember Peoples Name

Listen

Sincerely Make Someone Feel Important

Smile

Chapter 1: Why Should We Learn How to Read People Better?

"Life is about running your own car as it was built to be run,

plus getting along with the other drivers on the highway."

—Elsie Lincoln Benedict and Ralph Paine Benedict, lecturers and writers

It is human nature to seek to navigate the world better. This means knowing what makes people tick, both ourselves and other people.

If we think of ourselves as cars or motorcycles cruising along the road of life, it means knowing what types of engines or motors we have, what makes our engines run, knowing the rules and road signs, taking cues from other vehicles that we pass by, and putting these all together to help us navigate and reach our destinations or goals.

With this book as our roadmap, let us take the journey along the tricky and scenic roads of social navigation.

CHAPTER 2: Diving into the Human Mind

How We Perceive the World

Humans can be compared to living machines; we all gather information about the outside world, but we are all unique, which means we process and act on that information differently. Our brains work similar to that of computers, inputting truckloads of information in, processing it, and storing it in a plethora of ways, thus creating some sort of output. The core of the way we behave is due to stimuli that then produce responses; all while making connections inside our mind.

To have a reaction to the outside world, you must use one or all five of your sensory perceptions, also known as taste, touch, smell, hearing, and sight. These are responsible for feeding your brain with the right information to make appropriate decisions. You do not just see the world, smell the world, or hear what is going on, but your brain does too!

We stand out among the other living organisms in the world by our ability to sense the environment and then learn valuable intel from it and our experiences.

Feelings and Thoughts

Ah, human emotion. This is something that none of us can totally suppress, no matter how hard we try. This is one of the main reasons that receiving and providing feedback can be wildly challenging.

Back in the day, those who managed to survive constantly had their instincts, or emotional radars, on full blast. We used to have to trust our instincts for simple survival since we were susceptible to predators and other dangers. Fast forward to the world today, and instincts are still heavily prevalent, but in much different ways.

Many of us are taught to push back our emotions and instincts, especially when it comes to the business world. This is supposed to aid in business people utilizing their logical thoughts rather than acting on emotion along. But like I've mentioned before, you cannot totally hide emotion. This is why that despite the good news we hear, we often hear the not so great news the loudest.

These are just a couple examples of the exact reason why it can be difficult to read people. If you have folks in your personal and business life that are suppressing emotion, are you receiving the real version of them or a faulty one? This can greatly impact how we perceive and gather information about these people.

Habits

You can receive a lot of good intel from analyzing people from the way they act when they are the most comfortable. By observing their habits, one can distinguish many things. Habits are automatic actions we perform, which many times we do unconsciously. Many actions throughout an average day go completely unremembered. But the smallest of behaviors tell us how we approach life.

Here are some intriguing ways to decipher people's personalities as you are in the process of analyzing them:

Habits That Reveal Personality

Shopping Habits

☐ Des one look at all the ingredients on nutritional labels?

☐ Does one choose products quickly and without much thought?

Toilet Paper

☐ Is the roll over? Signifies dominance.

☐ Those that tuck the roll under are shown to be more submissive.

Eating Habits

☐ Slow eaters like to remain in control and appreciate life more.

☐ Fast consumers are goabriented, open to new things, and impatient.

☐ Adventurous eaters like to expand the boundaries of their comfort zones

☐ Picky eaters are neurotic in various aspects of life.

☐ Those who need to keep food separate are detail oriented and very disciplined.

Emails

☐ Take a closer look at your emails...

☐ Those with lower emotional intelligence tend to use more negative words.

☐ Narcissists tend to talk about themselves.

Punctuality

☐ Those who are regularly late are more laid back.

☐ Dreamers are overly optimistic.

☐ A perfectionist cannot leave till everything is back in order.

☐ The definer rebels against societal norms.

☐ Habits of Genuine People:

More often than not, people want to learn analyzing techniques to decipher if someone in their life is actually a genuine person. Here are a few tell-tale signs that those folks you are questions are indeed good people!

- ☐ Speak their mind
- ☐ Respond to internal expectations, not just external: What does this mean? It means that genuine folks spend quality amounts of time exploring their beliefs, expectations, and standards of life.
- ☐ Forget their paths: Meaning, they are more authentic, not dwelling on what people think or think they should be doing.
- ☐ Not afraid of failure: Genuine folks like to venture the road less traveled. They see failure as an important piece of the journey to becoming their authentic selves.
- ☐ Able to admit when they fail: They are true to their feelings, even the ones that might be difficult to admit, like failure.
- ☐ Don't judge: Genuine people realize that all people are on their own paths, experiences life is different ways. Instead of judging, they are accepting of the lives of others and encourage those around them to do their best.

☐ Have great self-esteem: Genuine individuals can absorb conflicts, criticism, and failures well. They are accepting of others and their successes, and not threatened by it. They are solely confident in what their life consists of and what they are working towards/have to offer.

I know what you are probably thinking: Why in the world is all of this information in this particular chapter together? It's simple really. All of it is connected. From the way in which we see the world around us, how we feel, act and react to outside stimuli, and the way we present ourselves via our habits and personalities, it is all connected as a great, thorough way to determine the type of person those in your life are!

Chapter 3: The Importance of Self-awareness

Self-awareness is a vital skill for personal development and good interpersonal relationships. It gives you a greater understanding of yourself and how you relate with others. When you are self-aware, you pay attention to your feelings, values, habits, personality, emotions, needs, strengths and weaknesses. It makes you take note of your reactions to the things that have a direct effect on you and the world around you. The knowledge of self-awareness can lead us to more life satisfaction, better life choices, and overall success, in both our private and professional fields.

Self-understanding enables you to know what is bothering you instead of being angry with yourself for just no cause. Furthermore, you will be able to guide yourself from taking wrong steps which can lead you astray because you will know exactly what to do and where you fit in life. Whether it's a career or a relationship, you will be able to know exactly where you should go without wavering.

Self-awareness helps you to know yourself well and trust your instincts more. You learn from the past, and you'll tend not to make the same mistakes over and over again. The knowledge helps you to put your emotion under control. You will be able to separate gut feelings from raw emotion and manage disruptive emotion positively.

Self-awareness can improve our sense of judgment and help us identify opportunities for professional development and personal growth. Having a perfect knowledge of who you are enables you to decide what you should do to improve for more exceptional achievement.

Self-awareness knowledge enables you to make peace with those who hurt you but to not give them the power to hurt you again. It will help you take positive steps towards happiness and personal satisfaction. You feel better instead of feeling that you are fighting an enemy that you don't know. When you hold on rigidly to past wrongdoings and pain you suffer in the hand of someone, you tend to miss trends of things and create tensions for yourself. Self-awareness helps you to be free and self-protective and operate within your limits. Understanding ourselves helps us to understand others better. When we are treated in a certain way by people, we can determine the underline factor for such behavior and know the appropriate thing to do to put the situation in control. We can choose not to be negatively influenced by the situation to effectively manage it.

No matter what your situation and what you desire of life the most essential thing in the world to any individual is to understand himself properly. This knowledge will help you to understand the people around you. As long as you cannot exist in isolation, understanding the other people around is crucial. Life is not a race you can run alone; other activities constitute vital obstructions along your pathway. You need to understand your own nature and the natures of other people. You may never get far without the collaboration, confidence, and friendship of other people around you.

Self-Awareness Improves Emotional Intelligence

Having self-awareness skills is crucial to developing emotional intelligence as a skill.Good knowledge of emotional intelligence will enable us to navigate through life social complexities without difficulties. When you become emotionally intelligent, you will be able to keep negative feelings and disruptive impulses under control, handle stress and channel positive and negative emotions innovatively. Developing emotional intelligence is about being aware of how we communicate with others. It can be a path to great accomplishment and happiness in life – especially in your line of business and at home. The ability to positively deal with people and manage relationships is essential in life, so enriching your emotional intelligence can be a brilliant way to show others the good qualities inside you. The level of your intelligent quotient determines your competencies and capacities, but your emotional intelligence determines how you manage your relationships with other people in your life, it shows how you are going to cope with pressures or handle stressful situations and make better decisions.

To a greater extent, life experiences are what we cannot control. But the good thing is that we can manipulate how, and to what extent circumstances affect us.

Emotional intelligence varies in individuals. To some, the slightest provocation will snatch their caution and put them off, while some will take a wilder and fiercer wind to be moved. However, being emotionally intelligent is not a gift, neither an innate ability nor a quality that requires to be transmitted genetically. Rather, it is something to be mastered and well understood; after all, the environment we dwell in is our teacher!

Emotional intelligence is a dynamic set of skills that can be acquired and enhanced with practice; you can develop strong emotional intelligence even if you aren't born with it. According to Howard Gardner, the influential Harvard theorist "Your EQ is the level of your ability to understand other people, what motivates them and how to work cooperatively with them."

Navigating through life social complexities takes tact and cleverness. Emotional intelligence helps you to understand and regulate emotion to handle life's obstacles and make the most of the situation at hand. The number of people you keep around will eventually depend on the amount of emotional intelligence you have.

People with higher emotional intelligence

- Easily maintain interpersonal relationships and feel comfortable in a group situation.

- Possess enhanced psychological state, which enables them to manage their stress positively.

According to a study carried out by the Social Behavioral Team at the University of Maryland, people with a considerable amount of emotional intelligence tend to be vast decision makers. They know when to rely on their intuition and focus solely on their power in handling stressful situations. They are more positive and harness the power from within, to tack and to prevail in all circumstances. The study concluded that people with high emotional intelligence extremely believe in themselves. They know their strengths and limits and can transmit such needs to other people effectively.

Learning diverse ways of showing emotions, using the right strategy to evade obstacles and effective response towards achievable goals require some decent amount of emotional intelligence.

Emotional Intelligence is vital because as individuals our success and the success of our career/work life today depend on our ability to read other people's signals and react appropriately to them.

You need to recognize your emotions, understand the language, and then observe how your physically displayed emotions influence the actions or decisions of others. Also, you need to focus on understanding other people's emotions, how they feel at the moment, and how you can use their feelings to create efficiency, leading to more significant improvement regarding your relationship with them.

To this end, it is essential that each one of us must develop the vital emotional intelligence skills necessary to understand better, empathize and negotiate with other people.

Chapter 4: The Alpha Male: How to Spot One

These are famous alpha men that many will recognize and know their alpha characteristics. You may imagine how it must be to have such presence and power. They are strong, interesting, intelligent, and have command of the room whenever they walk in.

Barack Obama

Brad Pitt

George Clooney

Bill Clinton

Denzel Washington

Clint Eastwood

Chuck Norris

Everyone is greeting each other and sharing pleasantries. While it is an enjoyable atmosphere, there is nothing exciting. Then, you notice an elevation of voices, greetings with a little more enthusiasm. In walks the alpha male. He has great posture. He stands straight when he walks. Notice how his shoulders are squared. His chest is raised but not puffed out. As he enters, he smiles when he greets someone and tilts his head slightly to show interest when listening. He reaches out and grasps your hand with a firm handshake. He has great eye contact. He knows how to maintain a persistent connection without looking away or downward. He is assertive and has a dominant persona. This guy has natural leadership skills; he just seems to flow without a struggle. He is courageous and appears to be physically strong. He is curious, ambitious, and independent. These are characteristics of someone we all know.

An alpha is aware that he is in command. He is not looking to impress anyone, except that special someone of the opposite sex. How can you identify the alpha in the room?

He is thronged by everyone around him. He is welcomed when he enters the room, and others offer him a seat. He draws attention and respect without utterance of words. Others may feel mediocre in his presence. The opposite sex is attracted to him.

President Barack Obama is an alpha male. When he stands before an audience, he stands with his feet slightly apart, and at times, places his hands on his hip.

This is a posture that's taking up space. With his hands on his hip and his elbows protruding outward, it gives him the appearance of being larger. This posture contributes to him standing erect and tall. His chest is pushed out and proud. His dominant posture is recognized by those around him. His body language says he is in charge, and everyone recognizes him as a leader.

How can you use your hands for nonverbal interaction? Gestures made with the hands can say a lot about you. A strong handshake is a symbol of strength. By extending the hand with the palm facing up sends the message of dominance, because your hand is on top which means you are on top. The palms facing up signify that you are asking for something or that you acknowledge the other person's advantage. When you clasp your hands together, it can be translated in a few different ways. It can mean that you are taking a posture of power or confidence, or it may also indicate nervousness depending on what else is happening at the time.

Hand gestures of leaders include steeple hands, when the fingers touch at the top and form a pyramid shape. Often, with the hand in front of the mouth looking as if in deep thought or concentration. This unspoken action transmits a confident and poised attitude. Ever notice the hands behind the back? This gesture, while it may be used in stressful circumstances when contemplating choices, portrays the authority look.

An Alpha male is assertive, not aggressive. He has a presence of refinement. He seems to be able to manage in any arena. He does not mind not always being right, but failure is not an option. He is very intelligent and knowledgeable. How others see him is not a major concern, because he believes in himself. He is aware of his abilities and is ambitious and a go-getter. As a gentleman, he can disagree without conflict, but he is not afraid of opposition. He is competent in his profession and aims to be the best. He does not have to blow his own horn.

He is admired by many and recognized for his excellence. He understands that much of the communication with him is through his body language. How you interact with others impacts how they respond to you. Your body will communicate things that you do not say in words. Studies have shown that more than 90 percent of communication is through body language. What you are saying is only a part of the communication process. Your expression, your tone, your eyes, and gestures are all just a part of the total conversation.

How do you take on these characteristics of an alpha male when you don't feel like one? You can change your situation and take control of how you are perceived. Here are a few key acts of a confident, poised, and powerful alpha male.

- Take up space
- Set feet about shoulder-width apart
- Stand tall and straight
- Shoulders back, chest forward
- Head held high
- Good eye contact, no looking down
- No fidgeting
- Do not cross arms
- No hands in the pocket
- Do not hold things in front as if to block
- Have an open position
- Face out to the room
- Walk slow and with purpose
- Do not rush or appear anxious

The alpha male is represented sometimes as aggressive and domineering. However, this is not an alpha male. He is not one who needs to tell others he is the alpha. A true alpha male knows who he is and his ability to influence others. He has a natural following of other males and the attention of females.

Consider the features of body language and how they influence your communication. Eye contact from an alpha male says that he is confident. It also lets the person whom he is looking at know that they have his attention. Their eye contact alone is not the total conversation. The face expresses how he feels or interprets what is being said. The face can say many things and may contradict the words that come from the mouth. As an alpha male showing strength, maintaining good eye contact is a must. Also, facial expressions should also convey the message of confidence and strength.

The posture of the alpha male is tall and erect, with shoulders back and head held high. His gestures should be at a minimum. No erratic movements. He lets every movement have a purpose. All the features of body language, while taken singly, may convey one message, but taken as a whole, make a totally different conversation.

It is normal for a man to desire to be an alpha male. How do you convert this desire into a reality in your life? One of the benefits of this conversion is being the prime focus of others in the group. Having a following of admirers, fans, and devotees is another desired benefit. The alpha male has the ability to draw and influence others. This is a powerful position to be in.

He has a charismatic flair which is influential to both men and women and is a crowd puller for those within and without his social circle. He has an alluring personality. Social preeminence is acknowledged by those in connection to the group and those outside the group. Prestige is associated with his presence.

They show devotion and camaraderie from others who follow. People tend to follow those who possess the in-charge personality. The attitude of devotion and camaraderie is proffered with availability for your desired purpose. He has the privilege of preference. This is the opportunity to be the first to enjoy privileges. Alpha males receive the privilege of having priority over others, being the first to partake.

He is also afforded the power to make decisions on behalf of the group. This includes both making the decision and having the first and final say in what is to be done. Much weight is given to his opinion. Everyone seeks his advice on what should be done, and when all has been discussed, looks for his opinion to finalize what will be done.

Becoming an alpha male does not just happen. There is some labor involved. To be the alpha, you must show that you have what it takes. You must exhibitsuperior qualities above others. Understand that, as with animal tribes, there is always one to challenge the alpha. He must be able to produce the characteristics that prove he's the alpha male. He cannot be intimidated by others and must show his strength and dominance.

In developing your "alphaness," consider the following suggestions:

Have Confidence: Know that you are the leader. Don't be anxious. If you believe in yourself, others will also. You must project this confidence. Don't wait for permission. Just do it.

Appearance: Be your best self. This is how you look and present yourself. Show your qualities as an alpha male. Be conscientious about your appearance. As a leader, your appearance should stand out as such. This includes how you walk, stand, grooming, body language, and clothes.

Be in Charge: Use your confidence and decision-making skills and take the initiative.

Respect: Be able to disagree and say so, but respect your opponent. You are no-nonsense and command respect from others. You do not withdraw from the encounter.

Boundaries: You know what is important. Making friends is not your first priority. Doing the right thing is the premier.

Listen: Hear what is being said and communicate.

Stand out: Be the life of the party. Be the person that stands out more than the others. Socialize with the gathering; introduce yourself to new people. Introduce those in your group. Participate in events at the function. Be outgoing and involved.

Watch others: If you want to learn how to be an alpha male, watch the actions of other alpha males and learn by example.

Work well with the opposite sex: Be confident and pleasant with women. Know how to interact appropriately without getting out of bounds. Understand the limits and boundaries. Be respectful and courteous.

Alpha doesn't say he's the alpha male. If you have to say you are alpha, you are not an alpha. Your presence will speak for you. Believe that you are and walk in that authority.

Temperament: Maintain control. Be composed. Don't castigate others. Knowing how to disagree and take control of situations are a part of the leadership quality of an alpha. Learn to demonstrate discontentment without being hostile or antagonistic.

An alpha male knows the power position. He knows where to stand and be seated to be in a powerful position. They are the head at the head of the table or the leader in the middle of a group setting.

Take stock of your strengths and weaknesses. Consider what message you are sending. Are you an alpha male, or do you want to be? As you read further, you will learn what it takes to become an alpha and how to do it. Alpha male personality traits include being assertive, dominant, a natural leader, protective, courageous, strong, and curious. Other characteristics include ambition, independence, sensitivity, presence, and being vocal, and competitive.

Chapter 5: The Basics of Body Language

There are many times that we give out more information with our bodies than with our words. We use our bodies to help us communicate well. Body language sends out non-verbal cues of what we mean when we speak. In short, it's a means to projecting how you feel without using words.

Body language involves more than just movement itself. It also includes a person's posture. So, when you are looking for those cues to see how someone really feels, it's important that you pay attention to posture as well as how a person moves (or doesn't move).

When it comes to body language you need to keep the five C's in mind. What do the five C's represent?

The Five C's of Body Language

1. Cues-Cues are an external event that cause us to perform a certain action or causes an internal response within us. It's important when reading body language to ask yourself the following question. What

just happened to cause that sort of response? Keep in mind that because cues are part of the conditioning of a person that not every person will react the same way to the same stimulus.

That's because we aren't all raised the same way. We don't all have the same reaction to the same situation. One good example of this is a war veteran. Those who return home with PTSD may react different to fireworks than someone who has ever gone overseas into a war zone. The external stimulation of the fireworks will cause (or cue) both people to have totally different reactions.

2. Change-It's very important that you pay attention to the transitions going on while you are observing others. When you notice a change in body language, you should think about the situation in reverse. Think about what just happened or what could have happened earlier in the conversation to cue the person's change in body language.

Knowing these changes can be very helpful when you are holding a difficult conversation with someone. You will know when it's time to stop or if the person is accepting the information that is being presented. Sales people watch for subtle changes in body language with their prospects. It's how they know that they can move forward and close the deal.

3. Clusters-Body language rarely occurs with just one motion. It often appears in clusters. That is, it often appears as a series of movements. These clusters can give you a better idea of what is going on within the person that you are watching.

These clusters most often send very clear signals about a person's meaning. Occasionally, the cluster movements will reveal a mixed signal to you. Pay special attention to the gut feelings that you have in these particular situations.

4. Character-It's important that you understand or at least know the basic character of the person you are talking to or observing. An extrovert may use more

grand gestures simply because they are outgoing. An introvert may use smaller gestures that are harder to notice.

You must include personality traits into your analysis. Temperament and mood can also affect their body language. Remember to account for those things as well. Everyone has acted in a certain way or said something while in a certain mood that they didn't mean and that is totally out of character for them. Keep that in mind.

5. Context-Like anything, it is important that you keep what you see in context. It's a bit like reading a book. To truly get the entire meaning, you must read a passage in its context. If you pull it out to stand alone, it often doesn't mean what the author intended.

Things that are going on in the surrounding environment can play a role in a person's body language. That is why you must pay careful attention to what is going on around you and keep in mind that other things such as anxiety, excitement and anticipation can play a role in a person's body language.

Chapter 6: What does body language entail?

Deborah Bull: "Body language is a very powerful tool. We had body language before we had speech, and apparently, 80% of what you understand in a conversation is read through the body, not the words."

Ever since the ancient of times, we have used our body language, in order to communicate, conveying our emotions and thoughts to those around us. Each person out there has a varied body language, encompassing not only facial expressions but also body postures and gestures. Even eye movement is considered as part of the non-verbal communication, being closely followed by touch and using one's personal spaces.

Body language, an integral element of non-verbal communication

As the above quote clearly points out, 80% of human communication is actually non-verbal. Some experts argue it may even be more. Body language is considered an integral element of non-verbal communication, being used, consciously or unconsciously, to interact with other people. It is often said that body language will serve to complement verbal communication; through our gestures, postures and expressions, we are actually transmitting a lot of information about ourselves to the interlocutor.

It is clear that the body language can make the difference between a successful interaction and one that is doomed to fail from the start. Basically, the information transmitted through non-verbal means, will ensure proper interaction between two or more people. However, due to cultural differences and other influencing factors, it is important to state that body language can sometimes lead to confusion or a state of ambiguity. One has to be able to use his/her body language to his/her own advantage, working at the same time to decipher the non-verbal information transmitted by the other person with utmost accuracy. In the end, by mastering the art of non-verbal communication, you will have more successful interactions with other people, reducing the risk of misunderstandings, confusion and social awkwardness.

How important are facial expressions?

Each person on this planet has facial expressions, commonly used to express emotions and/or thoughts. It is amazing how many muscles are involved in these facial expressions, allowing us to express our happiness, sadness or anger. Our eyebrows go high when we are surprised. We wrinkle our noses when something does not suit our preferences. The corners of our mouths go up when we are happy. An avalanche of facial expressions deliver information to the interlocutor regarding the way we feel or think.

Interestingly enough, we often use facial and bodily expressions at the same time, in order to convey a more meaningful interpretation of our thoughts and feelings. The person receiving the information will analyze both facial and bodily expressions at once, using his/her body language to respond to the situation in question.

The body posture serves to communication tremendously

A person's body posture can provide information regarding the way he/she is feeling. It is also useful for determining what that person thinks, at the moment in question. Bodily postures serve as a reflection of our emotions, whether we are aware of this for a fact or not. For example, if a person is sitting on a chair, with the back relaxed and arms and legs open, this means he/she is indeed relaxed, interested in communicating with the person standing in front of him/her. On the other hand, if the arms and legs are crossed, the interest in the said interaction is very low, if non-existent.

Even the smallest gesture matters

A wise person once said that small gestures can have a big impact. Throughout the entire day, we interact with a number of people, using gestures to complement our verbal messages. Our arms, hands and fingers move in various directions, as well as our head and legs. Most of these gestures are involuntary, but voluntary gestures can be used to highlight information that has been transmitted through oral means.

The gestures that we make can have a different impact, depending on the culture to which we belong. For example, many of the finger gestures are considered as acceptable in Western cultures and offensive in the Middle East. It is always important to take your time and determine whether a gesture is acceptable from a cultural point of view or not. In this way, you will ensure an appropriate interaction with the other person, without running the risk of being culturally insensitive.

What kind of information can gestures deliver? Well, let's take the hand gestures as example. If your hands are relaxed and moving openly, this means that you have confidence in the information you are presented and, of course, in yourself (self-assurance). On the other hand, keeping your hands clenched can represent that you are either stressed or angry. Constantly moving your hands or wringing them together can mean that you are agitated, nervous or anxious.

Handshakes, from ancient greeting ritual to modern times

History tells us that people started to shake hands, in order to demonstrate to others their peaceful intentions (and also the fact that they did not hide any weapons). Today, the handshake has become a common greeting ritual, helping one demonstrate the present level of confidence. A handshake can provide a lot of information regarding the person in question, especially when it comes to how willing he/she is to allow someone else in his/her personal space.

Handshakes can either be too weak or too strong, each situation conveying a different message about the person shaking those hands. If the handshake is too weak, this means that the person in question is not confident enough, being anxious or nervous with regard to the current interaction. A handshake that is too strong can mean a desire to dominate or over-confidence.

Cultural differences influence the meaning of handshakes as well. For example, in European countries, it is customary for men and women to shake hands, either as a greeting or as a form of agreement for a certain decision. In the Muslim countries, such an interaction is forbidden and severely frowned upon. Once again, we return to the idea of cultural sensitivity. We must always pay attention to culture and decide in an instant whether a certain gesture is culturally acceptable or not.

Food for thought

1)Analyze your body posture when you are meeting someone for the first time. Are you rigid or relaxed?

2)Find three gestures that bear a different significance according to the culture in which they are used.

3) How important are cultural differences when it comes to non-verbal communication?

Chapter 7: Introduction to Communication

People take food, water and shelter as the only necessities for life. However, there are other things that are just as important.

One of these is communication. Without it, we wouldn't know what to eat, where to find water or how to build a house.

What is Communication

Communication refers to an exchange of messages between two or more people. There is no way communication can take place if there is just a single person involved.

Talking, listening to the radio, seeing a road sign, looking at an ad in the newspaper etc. are all forms of communication.

One thing you must consider when sending your message is your channel of communication. Otherwise, your message might not make it to the receiver. For example, you would not make a phone call if you wanted to lecture someone. Rather, meeting in person would be your best bet.

At the same time, you must ensure that your message is clear to avoid confusing the receiver. Sending ambiguous messages is a violation of one of the most important rules of communication (although no one gets arrested for this crime).

When your receiver has got the message, he has a mandate to show that he has understood what you were trying to communicate. He may do this by nodding his head, replying through word of mouth etc. However, it is not every message that needs a feedback.

Types of Communication

From the definition above, it is easy to see that there are a number of ways you can use to communicate. However, we will only discuss the most common three:

1. Written Communication

As long as you know how to read and write, writing is one of the most common forms of communication you can use. It includes books, newspapers, chatting on social networks etc.

But being one of the most common forms does not make this type of communication superior.

It is only suitable in some situations. Its benefits are that you have a chance to rewrite until your message is clear. Additionally, it is easy to keep this kind of material for future reference.

2. Verbal Communication

This involves the use of voice to get your messages to the listeners. You can think of meetings, listening to the radio, talking face to face with a friend etc.

The best part with verbal communication is that feedback is instant. So if your message was not clear, you will have an opportunity to make corrections. Furthermore, you can deduce how the receiver has reacted to your message.

3. Body Language

One form of communication that is mostly ignored is body language. Although the body does not have a mouth of its own, it speaks volumes about what is going on in your mind.

Whether you want it or not, your body is always speaking. It's only when you are aware of what it is saying that you can take control and influence what other people make of your body language.

Examples of body language include clenching the fist when angry, rolling eyes, crossing arms as a sign of resistance, etc.

Chapter 8: Communicating with Body Language

We are constantly communicating, even when we are not speaking. Unspoken communication makes up over half of what we tell others and they tell us. It affects our work and personal relationships. Improves negotiating, management, and interpersonal skills by correctly interpreting body language and important signals.

Learning a New Language

In many ways understanding body language is like learning a foreign language. There are a few tips that make learning any language, even a nonverbal one, easier.

Tips:

Set Goals: Make sure that your goals are realistic and have specific timelines.

Devote time to learning: Schedule time to practice. Do not rely on spare time.

Practice daily: Hone skills by continued practice.

Enjoy the process: You are not in school. Relax and have fun with your new skill.

The Power of Body Language

Understanding body language does more than improve relationships. You will get insight into the thoughts and feelings of those around you. Because it is not a conscious form of communication, people betray themselves in their body language. Body language is powerful in several ways.

Power of Body Language:

It is honest: Body language conveys truth, even when words do not.

Creates self-awareness: Understanding body language helps you identify your own actions that hinder success.

Understand feelings: Body language shows feelings and motive such as aggression, submission, deception, etc. Use these as cues to your communication.

Enhance listening and communication skills: Paying attention to body language makes someone a better listener. Hear between the words spoken to what is being said.

More than Words

Much of the way people communicate is nonverbal. Body language specifically focuses on physical, not tone, or pitch. It includes the following characteristics.

Body Language:

Proximity: The distance between people

Positioning: Position of a body

Facial expression: The eyes are particularly noticed.

Touching: This includes objects, people, and themselves.

Breathing: The rate of respiration is telling.

Actions Speak Louder than Words

Our impressions of each other are based on more than words. People can have cordial conversations and not like each other. The actions that we take are stronger than our words. For example, a person may dismiss someone using body language and not saying anything negative. Like it or not, our body language makes a lasting impression on the people around us.

What Actions Can Say:

Deception

Confidence

Nerves

Boredom

Emotions

Attraction

Being open

Being closed off

Please note that this is not an exhaustive list of what body language can communicate.

Chapter 9: Types of Body Language

There are many types of body language we normally use and this is the basis on how we are seen by others. Following are the three components of body language and what it involves.

Facial Expressions

Your face is the most expressive and useful part when it comes to body language. It can tell your listeners a lot of things. Whenever your facial expressions change, you give your listener a chance to go into your world. Facial expressions are almost always universal. The expression for different emotions like happiness, sadness and others are the same even in different cultures. In fact, there are known facial markers that could express the truthfulness of your emotion. For example, a true smile often cause crinkles at the edge of the eyes while a fake one doesn't.

Body Movements and Posture

The perceptions of people vary depending on the way they sit, walk, stand-up and lift their head. The way you carry yourself gives your listener a glimpse of who you are. For example, if your shoulders are slouched, this can be interpreted as shyness and lack of confidence in your report. Straight shoulders and a direct gaze however are often seen as a sign of confidence.

Gestures

Your gestures may look normal to you but may look awkward for others. Hand gestures are commonly caused by complex thoughts which you can't translate into words. This is also a way of helping your listener follow the idea you are trying to explain.

Eye Contact

When you see something, it will also mean that you believe in it. That is why eye contact is important to most people. The way you look at each other in the eyes may mean a lot. It can mean that interest in both parties is developed, or it can also mean that you are both attracted to each other. It is also important in keeping the flow of your conversation and for predicting your listener's response.

Touch

Touch adds meaning to your words. For example, you need to congratulate someone for a job well done; it will mean more once you give a tap on the back. This helps in making personal connections and for touching someone's heart.

Space

Every person needs physical space. Not everyone is comfortable in being so close with you physically. But this may depend on the closeness of your relationship, your culture, or the situation. Space gives a variety of non-verbal communication such as signals of aggression, dominance, and intimacy.

Voice

When we say voice, it's not about the contents coming out of your mouth. It's about how you say it. Whenever we speak, some of the people read our voices. It can be the loudness or softness of your voice; it can be the tone, or the fillers such as "ahh" and "umm". A change in your tone may indicate that you are angry, being sarcastic or confident.

Chapter 10: Reading Between the Lines

Body language is just what the name reveals—the language of the body. It is a way of expressing what we think or feel through our unconscious or conscious movements and posture of the body, rather than with spoken words. But body language is much more than simply the way we move or hold ourselves. It also includes:

- The position of our bodies

- The facial expressions we make

- The distance between us and other people

- The way we touch ourselves or other people

- The way our eyes focus and move

- The contact our bodies make with other objects such as clothing, cigarettes, pens, etc.

- Other noticeable physical effects like heartbeat or breathing

Becoming able to read these signs that the bodies of other people reveal, is really not a rocket science; it simply means being perceptive. For instance, imagine a person giving a speech in front of an audience, but the people in the audience are hunched down and tend to observe their surroundings with their eyes, rather then focus on the speaker. A perceptive person will notice this and will see it as a sign that they are bored, so, despite the fact that he has a written speech, he may decide to go in another direction and throw some funny lines in, just to retrieve their interest and save the day. A nonperceptive person, on the other hand, will read his speech, thank the audience and return to his seat without impressing anyone. Now, what do you think, who will succeed more in life?Reading people's body language can be described as 'having a good intuition'. We have all heard of a'woman's intuition', but, does that has something to do with reading the body language? The answer is, absolutely. You see, unlike men, who were able to defend themselves, our female caveman ancestors were not that physically prepared to fight. So, their ability to read people (or their intuition) was really the only weapon they had. They were forced to observe everyone closely so they could avoid possible attacks. And although today, women are not facing physical attacks on a daily basis, the evolution has done its work and turned women into much more perceptive creatures than man. Like it or not, that is the reality.A certain study performed by the researchers at the Harvard University has supported this claim. The researchers gave the participants (men and women) to watch a short film and asked them to read the situations based on the actors'expressions. Women scored an amazing 87% accuracy, while men were only 42% accurate.

The Inborn Expressions

Some of the things that our body says are inborn and a part of the genetic character ofthe humankind. Charles Darvin was the first one to have found that, except for some extremely isolated tribes, all people have the same basic human emotions. I am talking about those expressions that even the least perceptive person can easily spot:

- Happiness
- Sadness
- Anger
- Fear
- Surprise
- Disgust

These six facial expressions are universal among all people and people's ability to express, as well as recognize them, is inborn.

The fact is that, up to a certain limit, we all try to interpret the other person's body language. And while we may succeed with the obvious signs, the humans are rather complex creatures that are capable of producing over 700,000 different movements. Incredible, right?But, before I delve deeply into explaining to you what different movements mean and how to analyze the other person the right way, I would like to point out that some of the people's movements (after all, there are so many of them), may be easily mistaken and interpreted the wrong way. Here is why:

The Context

It is extremely important that before you go on jumping to conclusions, to stop and think about the context of the given situation.You cannot read into the situation if you are unaware of the context. Know that some body language may be a result of something else. For example, if a person is keeping his arms crossed, that may not mean what you think it means. They may be as a result of the coldweather and the fact that the person didn't bring a sweater outside. Or, if someone is rubbing their eyes, that may not mean that they are tired or upset, it may be a result of an irritation or an allergy. Make sure to take all of the signs under consideration before you take the guess road.

The Evidence

Know that a single body movement or expression is a very poor indicator, and a really unreliable body language. You cannot judge or make assumptions based on one body language signal. For you to form an opinion, you must have a decent evidence to support it. Never think a certain way of someone just because he scratched his nose or closed his palms. You will need more than just one indicator to be able to rely on that intuition of yours. Always look for the clusters.If you think that a single body language signal means something, then if you are right, that signal will be accompanied by a series of other movements with similar meaning. Until that happens, you may be wrong. After all, you know they say—innocent, until proven guilty.

The Culture

As we said, certain expressions mean the same thing throughout the whole world, however, there is some body language that is specific to different cultures. And since we live in such mixed societies, it is extremely important to have in mind the cultural differences between different ethnical groups. Let's take the thumb-up gesture as an example. For instance, Italians use the thumb up when they mean 'one', while in the Western cultures, people use the index finger when they are referring to the number one. The Westerners use the thumb-up sign show that they agree with the other person. The Arab cultures find the same gesture to be rude.

The V-sign isn't any different. In some cultures, it may mean peace, to others victory, somewhere means simply 'two', whilst in Britain is considered something inappropriate.

The Relativity

Know that many of the body language signals are relative to gender and age. The gesture performed by one person in a certain situation may mean a very different thing when performed by another person in a different situation. When reading body language, you should also have in mind that younger people are far more energetic than older people, so understandably, they may display a lot more gestures.

Always have under consideration the type of person and the situation you are dealing with, before you make false assumptions.

The Faking

It is also important to know that some people intentionally make certain movements to send the body signals and create the impression that they want for other people to receive. They artificially control their body language, so it may be a little bit harder to read into such people, especially if you are a new 'reader'. However, don't get disappointed, since no one can completely fake their outward body language. The person may try to control the movements, but suppressing all of the outgoing signals is simply impossible. This is only another example why you should make assumptions based on a couple of body language signals but look for as many indicators as you can. The key lies in the tiny gestures. Mouth twitches, breathing, eyebrow raise, pupils contract, etc. can help you determine the correct outcome since these gestures are subconscious and uncontrollable.

Chapter 11: The Finale

I hope this book was able to help you to read a woman through her body signals while dating.Remember that women are not so obvious about how they feel because they are taking care of their pride. It is very possible that they give off signals that mean different things. Like you, they are also assessing every situation before showing their interest so they can avoid rejection. At the dating stage, it is highly discouraged that you ask her in words, if there is a chance that she is attracted to you. It poses a big risk on her end because she will be forced to assess how she feels and say it.

A woman is full of contradictions. She could show or say that she likes you, but every now and then she pulls away and her interest lessens. This is probably because she wants to know if you are interested in her beyond the sexual reasons. Because she longs for a serious and long-term relationship, she doesn't want to appear easy. She knows that if she plays hard-to-get, you will pursue her more. If not, then it only reveals that you are interested in a fling or a short-term thing. Hence, if a woman doesn't want a mere one-night stand, anticipate that her signals will be conflicting. Women also need reassurance. The reason why they are not sure if they like you is because they don't know if you will stick around. They are also concerned and afraid of expressing their feelings.

Conflicting signals mean that she shows both gestures of interest and disinterest. She can express interest with a direct eye contact and leaning towards you, but at the same time her arms are crossed. These mixed signals are very confusing and baffling. So what does this mean? As discussed in the previous chapters, each action means something. When combined, they don't form a new meaning. Rather, what you should do is analyze them independently and weigh if there are more counts of signals of interest. If it is half and half, then you should know how to adjust the results in your favor. She usually combines body gestures because she is not sure if you are interested in her too. So reaffirm her by also showing gestures of interest.

A woman is like a book. You should read her from start to finish. Take note of her body language before she approaches, when you start talking, and when you finish. Her signals could be positive at the beginning, and then take a negative turn somewhere in the middle. If you don't take the necessary measures, there will be no happy ending. This means that she doesn't really connect with you and she can't really relate to the topic that you've chosen. Maybe you talk more about yourself than asking about her. If she maintains the positive gestures all throughout, or probably let them become even more pronounced, then the two of you are clicking and your date might even have a sequel.

The next step is to use these types of body signals that you learned. You too can use body language to express your interest and to get women to reciprocate. Use your new knowledge to familiarize with her and to get closer to her. Depending on your end goal, whether it is just sexual intimacy or a long-term relationship, these tips will let you identify when the right time to move forward is.

Building a relationship takes time. And knowing a woman also takes time. Do not be impatient and immediately assume that she is disinterested. You could probably make the mistake of thinking that you are wasting your time on her. Give her time to know you better and give her enough space. Let her recognize that you also have feelings for her, but at the same time you also have your fears.

Last but not the least: practice, practice, practice. Like learning a new language, learning body language is also not that easy. These are simply the basic body languages of a woman, and it takes actual practice to really understand and eventually read her more accurately. Take one step at a time. Familiarize yourself with one gesture at a time and think about ways to react to them.

Through practice, you will also be able to differentiate if a signal means something or not. Most of our body movements are a result of habit; mannerisms that do not mean anything at all. If you prepare yourself in reading body language, you will be able to ignore meaningless body signals. Rather, you will only choose and absorb the ones that have an effect on your love life, at the proper time. And since you have more focus, you will be able to read women better. Dating is definitely a game, and knowing body language gives you the advantage. You can choose to win, change partner, or play an entirely different game.

Chapter 12: The Art of Subtle People Analysis

Most people who start studying personality types tend to become obsessed with the subject and start guessing the personality types of the people around them. If people start noticing that someone is analyzing them, they will begin to react differently. If this happens to you, you may ruin some relationships or you may get inaccurate results from your observations.

To avoid this outcome, you need to be subtle when observing people and their social behaviors. You can do this by using the methods in this chapter:

Gathering Information

When gathering information, you should first observe the appearance of a person. As discussed in the previous chapter, you can use this information as a clue to their judging versus perceiving preference. You can also observe them from a distance to guess whether they are extroverts or introverts. You can do this when observing them from a crowd or by initiating a conversation with them.

Take note of the way they look: what kind of clothes they are wearing, how groomed they are, and how they hold themselves up. People who look nice are often extroverts who care about what other people think about them. Those who are not that stylish or neat may be introverts who are more concerned with their own thoughts.

Observe their accessories. These will tell you stories about who they are and what they are interested in. A fondness for accessories and objects also suggests a sensing character.

When in a conversation, try to avoid guessing a person's personality type when you are still talking; this is the time when people tend to notice that you are observing and analyzing them. Try to gather and make mental notes of the person while you are talking. This is also a good opportunity to use a structured line of questioning in your small talk.

Using small talk effectively

Most people think of small talk as a waste of time but people in professions that constantly use this skill disagree. Lawyers, sales people and even doctors know that this is a great strategy to learn about their clients. When doing small talk, a person becomes more relaxed and is more likely to give natural answers. This is not the case when they feel that the other person is interviewing them. You're goal aside from gathering information is to make your target feel comfortable in talking with you.

• Create a structured line of questioning

In the 4 preferences criteria of the Myers-Briggs Type Indicator, you can easily guess whether a person is an introvert or extrovert easily by observing them or by asking people about them. You can also get a good idea of whether they are a judging type or a perceiving type by the way they look or by how organized they are. You can also ask people about them to learn about their thinking/feeling and sensing/intuition types. However, there are some areas where you will have very little information to use. You should limit your line of questioning on the areas that are difficult to guess in the person that you are trying to analyze.

You can use the example situations in the previous chapter in creating your questions.

- Establish a give and take interaction

Some types of people are not prone to giving personality clues in small talks. You need to make them comfortable with you before you can gain the information that you need. They will start becoming defensive if you are the only one asking questions. To make them more comfortable in giving away information, you should also answer their questions when they ask them. If they don't ask you questions, you can give answers to your own questions to start a conversation.

For example, when asking what color your target likes, you can say your own favorite color to increase the chance that they will answer your question.

● Remember their names and use it in the conversation

People are more likely to respond to conversations when you use their name. This is a good reason why you should pay attention to their name when they give it. If you didn't catch it the first time, you should not hesitate to ask for it because you have the intention of using it later on in the conversation. When asking the questions that you prepared, try to use their name somewhere in your question. This will increase the likelihood that they will take your question seriously.

● Look for a topic that they are interested in

You can easily know what the other person is into these days through what they share in their social media accounts. If you haven't done your homework or if you are doing an impromptu person analysis, you could ask them directly what they like to do on their free time. This information tend to be difficult to get out of introverts. If you believe that someone is an introvert, and you are having difficulty building rapport or gathering information on the other preference criteria, you should tell them about the introvert activities that you also do like reading books or playing video games.

- Create a conversation exit strategy

When you have all the information that you need from a person, you need to find a way to cut the conversation short to start your analysis. One way is to bring up that you are not feeling well and that you need to sit. You can also say that you need to do something or you need to talk to somebody else. The key to pulling it off is by selecting the right moment to bring it up. The best time to bring up your exit strategy is when the conversation is pauses when a topic is exhausted. This is the time when both you and your target pauses. Normally if you haven't collected all the information that you need, you could move to a different topic to have more opportunities to gather information.

Otherwise, you could take the pause as an opportunity to use your exit strategy.

Organize the information and apply them in each preference criterion

After gathering information about your target, you should try establishing their preferences. For example, you should ask yourself whether they are extroverts or introverts and give evidences for your answer through the information that you gathered. You can do the analysis in each of the criterion. If you are not sure in some areas, you can check the person's social media account or go have another conversation with him or her.

Go back to the Keirsey Temperament Sorter

As a beginner, you need to refer to the Keirsey Temperament Sorter constantly after knowing the type of your targets in each of the four-preference criterion. Some personality types occur more often than others. As you analyze more people, you will become more familiar with the more common types. Only then will you be able to read people accurately as you meet them. For now however, you should go back to the descriptions of each personality type every time you make an analysis.

Chapter 13: Reading People Through Their Words

They say that the eyes are the windows to the soul and that words are the gate way tothe mind. Words express thoughts. Listening to the words that a person says or writes is the closest one can get to understanding someone else's thoughts. Some words also reflect the behavior of a person.

Word clues build up the chance of anticipating people's behavioral characteristics by studying the words they choose to say or write. Although these words alone can't determine the personality traits of a person, they can give insights into his thinking and behavior. Assumptions can be formed based on word clues and then use additional knowledge obtained from the person to test it.

People only use nouns and verbs when thinking. The other parts of speech are included when thoughts are transformed into written or spoken language. A simple sentence is made up of a subject and verb. For instance, "**I ran.**" Words added to this sentence structure changes the quality of the subject and the verb. These conscious changes give behavioral and personality clues of a person. Added words show who we are and what we're thinking.

With the help of word clues, observers can come up with educated guesses or assumptions about other people's behavioral characteristics. For example, "**I ran quickly.**" The word quickly instills urgency, although it didn't give any reason for it. It might indicate that a person is late for a meeting or appointment.

Diligentpeople view themselves as dependable and thus, they don't want to run late for anything they think is important. They respect social standards and try to live up to other people's expectations. These people are usually considered to be good employees. People may add words for different reasons, but there's a specific reason behind their choice.

Word clues show a non-invasive way to read people effectively even without them knowing. Below are some examples showing how word clues give insights about people's personality and behavior.

I worked hard to reach my goal.

Adding the word **"hard"** implies that goals which are not that easy to accomplish are important for the person. The goal he achieved may be much more difficult compared to his other goals in life. The word might also indicate that the person can put off gratification or believes that dedication and hard work yield good results. If you're an employer, you may consider that applicants who possess these certain characteristics would probably make a great employee because they are determined to successfully complete any tasks they take.

I sat patiently during the lecture.

The word **"patiently"** suggests various hypotheses. The person might have been bored throughout the lecture. Maybe he needed to go to the restroom. Perhaps he has an important phone call to make. No matter what the reason is, the person was concerned with something more urgent than the lecture. Someone who patiently waits for a break before leaving the room is likely to follow social rules and standards.

On the other hand, when a person instantly gets up and leavesthe room when his phone rings probably doesn't have strict social limits. People who have established certain social boundaries can be regarded as good employees since they respect the rules and authority. Meanwhile, a person who doesn't like following social practices are more suitable for jobs that require innovative thinking. People who tend to act beyond social norms are more likely to become better spies because they are often asked to go against social standards.

I won another award.

"Another" is a word clue that expresses the idea that the person may have won previous awards. He makes sure that other people are aware that he won an additional award. This way, he tries to boost his self-image. Perhaps he needs other people to admire him increase his self-esteem. Observers can use this weakness by throwing compliments and other self-enhancing remarks.

Listening to People's Voice Tones

Vocal qualities play a vital role in finding out what a person is saying. You can learn about a person's feelings by means of his voice. In some cases, these traits bear hidden messages that force you to listen.

The volume and tone of voice can say many things about a person's emotions. Pay attention to inconsistencies in terms of pitch or tone. Sound frequencies produce vibrations. Are they happy and furious at the same time? There's a possibility that they're trying to hide something. Do they talk quieter or louder than usual? A person speaking with a loud voice might suggest that they need to manage the situation they're in. They make use of their voice to control and threaten, like that of a drill instructor.

Other times, they might simply be trying to make up for something they seem to lack. A person talking with a loud voice could also indicate that he has a poor sense of hearing or probably drunk. You need to consider every possibility. A soft voice could also have several meanings. It doesn't necessarily point out that a person lacks confidence, though.

Maybe they're just feeling tired or downhearted. It may also suggest that they are self-assured. A soft voice may even express their arrogance in a way that you need to listen closely if you want to grasp what they're trying to say.

When analyzing people, you also need to observe how their tone affects you. Does their manner of speaking feel reassuring? Is it harsh, abrupt or complaining? Notice the length of their responses. Short and clipped answers could mean that a person is busy or frustrated. Long responses might tell that he is happy and interested with the conversation.

Consider all the probable explanations for mumbling, various emphasis, and intonations, slow or rapid speech, a flashy, whiny, or unemotional tone of voice. Listen to what people say and allow their words to do the talking. They may bring out something deeper than what you initially expected.

CHAPTER 14: USING BODY LANGUAGE EFFECTIVELY

People may be dishonest in what they say but facial expressions and other body language tend to be more telling. When a person's words and body language are consistent, we believe that person.

When their words and body language say different things, we tend to believe the body language and doubt the words. Bottom line. You need to be cognizant of nonverbal communication and how to use it to your best advantage to be an effective communicator.

Using Body Language Effectively

Always be as aware of a person's body language as you are of the words they speak. When you first meet someone, it is not unusual for them to appear nervous or reserved. This makes sense.

After all, they don't know you and don't know what to expect. If you have perfected your nonverbal communication you will most likely be able to set them at ease. As a result they will tend to display more open body language.

If someone responds positively to you, you know you are on the right track. If you sense a negative reaction you should change gears and modify the direction you are headed in. Try to figure out what the problem is to determine how to proceed.

Try asking open-ended questions to increase involvement. Focus on the other person's interests. Figure out something you have in common to establish increased rapport before moving ahead.

Being an Effective Listener

Lean forward slightly. If you lean backward the other person may be confused. Are you comfortable or distracted? Are you simply relaxed or are you being disrespectful?

Pay attention to your posture. It speaks volumes. Don't slump. It's unattractive and riddled with negative nonverbal cues. If you are seated, sit up straight and leave your arms and legs uncrossed. If you are standing, don't lean against walls or doors as if you cannot support yourself. Refrain from constantly shifting your body weight from one foot to the other. It's distracting.

Be attentive and try not to fidget. Don't finger your jewelry, hair, clothing, or anything in your pockets. It suggests boredom and impatience with the speaker or the topic. Either way, it is unattractive.

Maintain good eye contact. It says you are paying attention. It says you are interested. It says you want to be there. Avoid staring, however. It will only make others uncomfortable.

Be aware of what you are doing with your arms and hands. If you fold your arms in front of you others may interpret this to mean you are unreceptive. Resting your clasped hands in your lap suggests you are critical of what is being said. Can't you just picture someone doing this with pursed lips?

Nod your head from time to time. It lets others know that you are actively listening.

Be an Effective Speaker

Face the person you are addressing. Sitting at an angle or facing away from someone suggests you are not interested. It may also make you look rude.

Use a conversational tone. Change the pace at which you speak occasionally to maintain interest. Place emphasis on certain words and phrases to underscore important points you are making. Use pitch and volume to your advantage. And don't race through what you have to say. You will appear to be nervous.

Stand about two feet away from the person you are talking to. It's a distance you should both feel comfortable with. Standing closer will make the other person feel as though you are encroaching on their space which triggers defensiveness. Standing further away is awkward and will make the other person question how you feel about them.

Use gestures to emphasize the points you make but limit the space in which you make them. Avoid pointing at anything or anyone especially the person you are talking to. It is not only bad manners, it is aggressive and will not be well received.

Chapter 15: The History and Background

Scientists and philosophers have seen the connection between physical behaviour in humans with personality, mood, and meaning for many centuries, but body language has been a much more recent study. We have a long way to go with this sect of psychology, though it has become quite detailed and sophisticated when compared to older times. Recorded studies and research on this subject are either limited or non-existent until the middle of the twentieth century.

The First Thinkers to Consider the Subject:

The first experts we are aware of to contemplate this subject were the ancient inhabitants of Greece. Aristotle, Hippocrates had an interest in behaviour and the personality of the individual. We can also assume that ancient Romans had an interest, and Cicero in particular, who enjoyed contemplating communication and feelings of humans. A lot of this interest in related subjects had to do with developing ideas about speech and oration, due to how significant this medium was for government and leadership in ancient times.

In more recent eras, written material on body language has appeared. We can look, for example, to the year 1605 at the works of Francis Bacon, where he reflected on the way gestures are an extension of verbal conversation. An author named John Bulwer published a book about hand gestures in the year 1644, and in 1806, Gilbert Austin explored the effectiveness of improving speech with gestures.

Experts on Body Language:

Darwin in the later part of the 19th century was the earliest influential academic figure to have observed body language in a serious and scientific manner. However, ideas in this area seem to have slowed down or possible halted altogether for the next century and a half.

The work of Charles Darwin opened the door to a lot of ethological schools of thought, some of which started with studying the behaviour of animals. In the early twentieth century, it was established, and then grew to cover the behaviour of humans and the organization of social structures increasingly.

In the areas that ethology covers the evolution and communication of animals, the study strongly relates to the body language of humans. Ethologists have proceeded to apply the knowledge gleaned from these studies to body language, looking back the early origins of unspoken communication. Similar to psychology, ethology is a wide and varied science which continually clarifies our understanding of nonverbal communication and all it entails. The academic understanding of body language, in an accessible and popular format, is relatively new.

Julius Fast published a book on the subject in 1971 and commented that the science is so young that its experts are virtually unheard of. Fast was an award-winning author from America who published both non-fiction and fiction, focusing mainly on human behaviour and physiology. His previously mentioned book was unique in that it was one of the first published works to introduce the subject of body language to wider audiences.

Although Fast was among the first, a few exceptions exist, such as Charles Darwin, who was a major influence to the author. Darwin published a book in 1872 which directly discussed emotions in animals and men. This work was among the first works published about the science of body language, even though it wasn't recognized that way until later on.

Early Psychologists Touching on the Topic:

In the later years of the 1800s, as well as the earlier parts of the 1900s, others would contemplate aspects of body language, such as Freud and other academics in the psychology field. These experts had an awareness of body language aspects such as personal space, but hardly ever focused directly on unspoken communication or came up with their own theories about the concept of body language. At the time, psychologists (including Freud) were focusing on analysis for therapeutic reasons and behaviour studies, much of which didn't see body language studies as necessary.

A book called The Naked Ape came out in 1967, published by Desmond Morris, which covered new visions of human behaviour studies and touched on body language topics. The author was a zoologist from Britain and was fond of writing about human behaviour and the way we communicate to the animalistic side of human evolution. The work of this author is still popular today, though slightly controversial, and can shed a lot of light on the way humans behave.

Even though Desmond Morris' books didn't directly mention or strongly focus on human body language, how well-received the author was had a lot to do with people's interest in the subject increasing. For the first time, widespread interest in body language had stretched beyond the scientific community and people were becoming more curious about the way we communicate with one another beyond words.

Facial expressions are arguably one of the most important aspects of body language, but it's difficult to trace scientific studies done on it in early times. However, some information exists on the topic.

Body Language Definitions:

<u>Physiognomy</u>: This is a related and quite obscure definition in the study of body language. The word describes expressions and facial features which have been considered to indicate an individual's ethnic origins, nature, or general character qualities.

The old roots of this word show that, although the idea of body language as a concept is a newly defined method of analyzing psychology, the concept of inferring character and the nature of an individual from expressions of the face is no new idea.

<u>Proxemics</u>: Earlier we briefly touched on the idea of personal space. Proxemics has been used as the technical definition to

describe this concept. This word has been around since the mid-1900s and was developed by an anthropologist using the word for nearness or closeness; proximity.

<u>Kinesics</u>: This term is used to describe the interpreting of communication using the motions of the body. This can refer to any behaviour that is unspoken, uses movements of body parts or the full body, gestures, or facial expressions.

Chapter 16: Non-verbal Communication

There's a line from a country western song that says "You say it best when you say nothing at all." While this may be an exaggeration where expression of what humans are internalizing is concerned, there is truth to the notion that subtle innate cues can be suggestive of what we are thinking how we will interact with others. Things that people would never tell us or openly reveal about themselves can be derived by being alert to the presence of these tell-tale clues.

Body language, that is our movements and mannerisms that are gestures reflecting our thoughts and feelings is a tremendously revealing form of communication. This kind of expression is among the most reliable and honest of indicators of what is going on within us because it is innate in its very nature. We don't give thought prior to emitting these largely involuntary signals. This can render the words we use as meaningless or suggest that we're not being very truthful. It is helpful to observe your bodily response to what you are saying. Does your body language suggest the confidence that you are trying to come across within your commentary? If the two are inconsistent, it may compromise the message you are trying to deliver.

When you're meeting someone for the first time, body language is perhaps the most powerful analytical tool you can employ. Your inherent lack of familiarity means that you don't know their trends and tendencies where verbal communication is concerned. They could be purposely reserved given your status as a stranger to them, or there might be something that they just do not want to share. Their gestures and movements will be a reliable indicator of what they're thinking. Their posture, expressions, and the distance they maintain from you will tell you something, even though the person may say very little at all. Even if the signals they emit suggest nervousness, apprehension, or some other concern, this can be used to your advantage. Sensing this, you can rescue the interaction by bringing calm or resolve the situation.

Once we have familiarity with others, we can inventory their behavior and movements of expression over time and have an appreciation of trends and patterns that generally repeat themselves. For example, if someone exhibits a particular posture when they are nervous about something or if they cast their eyes downward when they're disappointed, this may signal to you the need to come to the rescue. It allows you to take the opportunity to tactfully inquire as to what might be bothering them. As time goes on, you will be able to use these patterns to your advantage in making communication more productive as you associate them with particular emotions or feelings the person has inside.

One nuance to using body language to assess others' feelings is that there are cultural differences and in today's world of global travel and increased interactions with those from different cultures it is valuable to learn what these are, particularly if you are going to place yourself in another country or region of the world. Here in the United States, people of European descent tend to look one another in the eyes when speaking to them, whereas indigenous Americans or Native Americans tend to not look someone in the eyes when speaking as this is considered invasive.

Body language is a great way to start analyzing the behavior of others, particularly those with whom we lack familiarity. It is not a stand-alone metric and, ideally, is employed in combination with other techniques for a complete assessment possible. It does allow us to use subtle gestures to make an initial determination without coming across as probing or prying into feelings that others may not want to openly express. As you pay more attention to the signals others are sending your way, it should also make you more conscious of what you may be sending to them. Take inventory of yourself just as you would of others. You have control over what you communicate to others, but much less over what they send to you.

The distance someone maintains between someone else and themselves can reveal something about the closeness of the relationship between the two. If people are physically contacting each other or within 1.5 feet, this indicates an intimate relationship such as a romantic partnership. If the standing distance is 1.5-2.4 feet, then they may be considered to be close relatives or friends. Four to 12 feet would suggest familiarity, but nothing beyond being acquainted with each other. If a distance beyond 12 feet is maintained then it is likely that there is no level of personal connection and this reflects the distance maintained by members of the public at large. Context is important here of course, and these generalizations must be qualified given the situation at hand. People who do not know each other can get in each other's face if they've come into contact as the result of a fender-bender. Those who do know each other may keep at a greater distance from one another when they're frustrated with one another.

Eye contact and eye movement tell us much because of the strong sensory information that our eyes are designed to gather. Pupil dilation or changes in the size of the pupil can indicate emotions associated with apprehension or frustration. While natural chemicals, specifically hormones such as oxytocin are released into our bloodstream during moments when we're highly aroused (such as when faced with a 'fight or flight' response), contribute to pupil dilation, drugs, and other synthetic chemicals can do this as well. As previously implied, eye contact is culturally-dependent, but generally downcast eyes suggest respect but can also reveal embarrassment, fear, or guilt. If someone looks up for a brief period, they may be disinterested or trying to recall something. Side-to-side movement may indicate a lack of honesty, lost interest, or simply distraction. Gazing and staring are distinct ways in which we look at others that reveal particular emotions. A gaze is an extended look at someone lacking the intention of provoking a reciprocated look that implies sexual attraction or great interest. Staring is a period of prolonged exchange of eye contact that is very context-dependent as it occurs with a wide range of intense emotions being shared. People will stare at each other out of anger or tremendous affection, as different as these may be. If we glance at something or someone, we are giving a brief look that indicates interest or contemplation. We might be curious about something or we may be considering making a critical move and weighing the consequences, such as making an introduction or embracing someone. Closed eyes first and foremost tell us that the other person feels the need to end communication for the moment. They may be signaling a need for more time to respond, or that they are feeling embarrassed or angry. When we follow the movements of others, we can be interested in a variety of reasons ranging from being favorably interested to apprehensive about them. Winking at someone can be interpreted as either joking or kidding in many cases, but it is also a signal of affection. If we're sarcastic, angry, or unsure about something we may cast an extended look at someone and blink our eyes during a verbal exchange.

Eye movements may be accompanied by contraction and relaxation of muscles associated with the face produce what we refer to as facial expressions. Smiles can send mixed signals, although a fully engaged smile with raised cheeks and open lips can generally be regarded as positive, whether it is happiness or varying degrees of pleasure. Alternately, a wry smile is usually an expression of politeness or sarcasm. When we're saddened or upset it is a little more obvious. Our eyes narrow and the corners lack the wrinkles observed when we are smiling. The corners of the mouth are turned down, our lips are closed, and the lower lip may protrude to one degree or another. When we have strong feelings of disdain for something, we squint our eyes and our lips are closed and drawn up and if our pigmentation is light our complexion may intensify. If we find something repulsive or unpleasant in taste, our eyebrows will constrict, our muscles constrict giving our nose a scrunched appearance, and our upper lip will curl upwards. Eyes wide opened with raised eyebrows can indicate fear or shock. An expression of anger or hostility consists of eyebrows being drawn down and toward the center. Depending on the degree of which the person is upset, the lips may be opened or closed and this expression is often accompanied by heavy breathing.

Posture, or the way someone positions their body, can tell us much about how that person feels toward us or how they feel in a certain situation. If someone is standing straight with shoulders widened, they are communicating authority or extreme confidence. If someone is in a lowered position, whether sitting or squatting, it can suggest submission or humility. If someone is leaning over with slumped shoulders, it indicates dejectedness or a low-energy level.

Movements of the head are pretty reliable. A side-to-side shaking of the head may indicate amazement or disbelief at what is being observed. Nodding of the head indicates agreement. Tilting of the head indicates contemplation or uncertainty.

Lots of people are said to talk with their hands. These are usually high-energy folks that are confident and convincing with what they have to say. Since their words usually corroborate this, the hand gestures are primarily for emphasis.

Crossed limbs are often interpreted as a sign of disagreement or being unreceptive toward others, but this conclusion must be taken with caution as some people are more comfortable sitting with their legs crossed or if they are slightly chilled, may cross their arms to reduce the loss of body heat.

Involuntary shaking or trembling of lower extremities usually indicates nervousness or an elevated energy level, the latter being related to restlessness and an associated lack of focus. This may be accompanied by appeasement behaviors such as grooming, doodling on a piece of paper, or picking at loose threads on clothing.

Believe it or not, people even pay attention to how well we listen. They notice when we are distracted or disinterested and this affects their image of us in some way, usually not in a way that is favorable to us. When folks do not perceive that we are giving them our attention it can suggest to them that we are arrogant, of greater importance than themselves, or that we are a poor candidate to conduct business for the company. When we are speaking to a group we generally have the expectation that the individuals have an interest in what we are sharing with them. It is reasonable to for them to expect as much from us. There are several tips to being what is referred to as an effective listener. One way to demonstrate effective listening is to ask questions or respond to questions by the speaker when prompted. Perhaps questions are only invited at the end of the presentation, and if so be ready. During the presentation, exchange eye contact with the presenter. If you're constantly looking somewhere else when they cast a glance in your direction, this will make the speaker feel as though they were not worth your time. When a speaker recognizes that you are aware of what they are saying, it suggests you are open-minded and persuasive. If the point of the talk is to sell you on a new idea, you should appear to be listening just so that you will be deemed a thinking individual with whom they would want to engage with on other potential opportunities in which collaboration is possible.

Good listening skills are not just important when we're in the audience at a talk, as productive conversations require the same abilities. One difference is in conversations, we may also need to be conscious of any tendency to interrupt or cut someone off as they're speaking. It is rude and suggestive of self-importance. When the other person has finished speaking, we can respond or proceed to communicate what came to mind. If there is a desire to change the topic or make a transition in the conversation the person switching the topic should bring the discussion of the previous topic to a conclusion and then proceed to the next subject. Also be mindful of speaking volume and tone. Don't speak so loudly that the other person thinks you are trying to dominate them. Speak at a constant level of volume adding inflection and pitch to your tone of voice when appropriate. If you speak in a monotone, the more important points you have to make may get lost as they do not stand out relative to supporting details.

Finally, a word of caution to the observer that it may be necessary to look twice or more deeply to make sure that emotions are not confused where non-verbal communication is concerned. Context is usually important here. Facial expressions suggestive of confusion could possibly be mistaken for anger. Smiles may be exaggerated, even when feeling sarcasm and discernment is often achieved by accompanying comments. Usually, multiple non-verbal signals are being simultaneously emitted and the whole picture must be taken into account to determine what emotions are being communicated and in some cases, there will be multiple emotions, particularly in unexpected situations that take people by surprise. And we must not forget that there is often a cultural context to non-verbal communication. As the old adage goes, when in Rome…

Chapter 17: Practice Makes Perfect

Body language has its roots in differentiating between cultures. From the great story in the Bible of the Tower of Babel, all the way to modern-day interpretations of body language that vary from country to country, body language has often been how others read an individual's true intentions.

The types of bodily cues found in the Western world do not mean the same things as they do in the Eastern cultures. When people were beginning to migrate and travel, many thousands of years ago, they relied on their interpretation of body language and nonverbal cues to determine whether an indigenous people were hostile to another's presence. Because they could not communicate verbally with all the different languages in play, many individuals became very adept at interpreting body language, in order to keep their tribe safe during travels.

Now, reading body language and nonverbal cues serves many different purposes. Police officers interpret them when interrogating subjects, lawyers pay attention to it when cross-analyzing witnesses on the stand, mothers use it whenever they are raising their children, and even friends use it to interpret the emotional impact of an event on someone they care about.

Analyzing people is equal parts body language, speech, nonverbal cues, and environmental. All of these things play together to give someone the greatest possible chance of interpreting someone, how they are feeling, and what they are thinking.

Getting better at analyzing and reading people is a matter of practice. As you continue to watch people and draw your own conclusions, the scenarios you find yourself in will either reinforce or disprove the theories you concoct in your head. Part of getting better at this skill is simply doing it. Also, part of getting better at this skill is memorizing what you are looking for, so you know what type of label to put to it.

This book outlines the latter, and it is your responsibility to enact the former.

One of the most important things you can do for your journey is to get over your own personal biases. Whether you are aware of them, or whether they are unconscious, predetermined emotional and personal biases will skew your results and your observations every single time. However, there are a few things you can start doing to help get over those biases, whether you believe you have them or not.

If, for some reason, you feel you are free of personal bias completely, just indulge me for a moment and implement a few of these tactics anyway.

The first thing you can do is intentionally introduce yourself to things that go against those modern-day stereotypes. Do you believe all Californians are surfer dudes with blonde hair and no brains? Then find a girl from California who is attending school and hates the ocean. They exist, and they exist in droves. Strike up a conversation with them and get to know them. Don't try to analyze and don't try to label. Just... take it all in. Use it to reconstruct your opinion of "Californians."

Do you believe people from the South have thick accents, wear cut-off t-shirts, and hate black people? Then sit down with a Native American southern Methodist pastor in one of the southern-most states and get to know her. Ask her questions about her faith and beliefs. Willingly introducing yourself to people who do not fit the "molds" you have conditioned yourself to believe, will help burst those personally ingrained biases you already have.

Another way to bust those personal biases is to volunteer in your community. For many, personal biases are formed when they stick with what they know: the same types of people with the same types of careers who speak the same type of language. Get into your community and volunteer some of your time at a shelter.

Maybe there is a YMCA program that invites disenfranchised youth over after school for programs until their parents get off work. Maybe there is an after-school center that runs off volunteer tutors. Get into those areas of your community you are not familiar with and immerse yourself in their world.

Sometimes busting your own biases simply means exposing yourself to other parts of the world around you... even if that world is simply 10 miles downtown.

Another way to burst those personal biases is to find people who are outside your social circle that you admire. Every single group of individuals has a figure they look up to. The issue is, those groups usually never intermingle, so those revered individuals never get the chance to break down walls we naturally throw up to separate ourselves. Maybe this admired individual has not done anything to personally help you and your situation, but you can still admire them for their words and their actions.

Find someone admired in the community who is wholly different than you. Maybe they have different political views or religious beliefs. Maybe they come from a different ethnic background or country, or even speak a different language. Expose yourself to them and work to find out why they are so respected within their community.

It will not only give you a way to cross those natural walls we all create, but it will give you a chance to admire someone you might have otherwise passed by.

Just like learning how to analyze people properly takes time, so does getting rid of personal biases. For many, these biases are learned as children and then reinforced by media and entertainment outlets that their family units habitually consume.

As a child, this is not something you can control. As an adult, however, it is your responsibility to take whatever action is necessary to destroy your own biases, should they be stepping in your way.

Different cultures, when intermingling with one another, rely heavily on bodily language as well as nonverbal cues in order to understand one another. Body language is first used to determine whether an individual is hostile, and then it is used to determine if the newcomer is welcome. When both of those initial assessments move in a positive direction, then analyzing someone becomes less about safety and more about learning about the environment around them.

Learning to analyze people is not simply about trying to figure out who is lying or who is telling the truth. Learning to analyze people is also about being respectful of other customs. It is a skill that will always require new inputs of knowledge as you are exposed to other people and cultures, and it will always be a skill that will never be 100% accurate.

But, learning how to more accurately analyze people will always give you the edge, no matter how you choose to implement the skill.

Chapter 18: Well Armed

Arms are like barriers, they can be open or closed.If they are in an open posture then the person is indicating that they are responsive, open and secure.If the arms are in a closed posture then they are very defensive and switched-off to ideas and interaction.

Arms folded across the chest are an indicator of negative feeling, a defensive or defiant attitude. It indicates that the person is uncomfortable in the situation. A more intense version of this posture occurs when the hands are in a closed fist position.This can indicate a very hostile attitude.If the person grips their upper arms they are quite literally holding on to that attitude and will try to resist change.

A less obvious defensive pose consists of a partial arm cross where only one arm covers the body and the other hangs down by the side of the body.

Frequently, just before I take the stage, whether in performance or in the delivery of a keynote, I catch myself adjusting and re-adjusting my cufflinks and shirt cuffs. I am in fact bringing my arm across my body to do so, subconsciously seeking protection from my audience.

Arm barriers can take on many guises some more subtle than others. Inanimate objects around the home and office can also be used to create a subconscious barrier. Things like clipboards, books, magazines, document folders and coffee cups can all be used to keep people at a distance both physically and mentally.

The workplace is a great place to watch out for office arm blocks.You'll also suddenly be aware when you are using your own blocks either with just your arms or by holding a prop of some sort.

Chapter 19: Body Language

Body language is one of the most significant indicators of human emotion and expression. Knowing how to use it properly can help you be perceived differently and taken more seriously. It can also help you understand what other people think or how they're feeling. Nevertheless, it must be noticed that some people have mastered the art of body language and are able to use it to hide their emotion and put on a "mask". Having this in mind, body language can't be your only way of understanding people (there are other ways which will be discussed later on in this book), however, it can still help you a ton and be a great starting point.

The basics of body language can be broken into four categories (each one will explained and elaborated later on in this chapter). The first one is the appearance of the person. Different clothes and accessories convey different messages. We'll discuss which style is best for being taken seriously and what are the different occasions where specific styles should be used. The next one is posture. Standing up straight can help you a lot with looking more confident and calm. Hunching over may make you look like you're lazy, shy or even both. I'll tell you the exact way to position your body, along with the many benefits. Following this, we have physical movement, such as: crossing arms, lip biting, distancing etc... This can be extremely helpful with understanding women and improving your dating game. Additionally, it can also help you convey a message without using your tongue. The fourth section is the facial expression. As with clothes, different facial expressions signal different feelings and intentions. By reading this, you will understand while smiling/frowning all the time isn't right and how it can impact your first impressions.

To give you a quick example of why body language matters, I will put you in a real life scenario. Imagine two people, both of which have an intention of selling you something. The first one is dressed in a clean, ironed suit, while the second one wears baggy cargo pants, along with an old t-shirt. The second one may have better selling skills or a better product, but upon your first impression, you'll most likely prefer the first one. The same goes for the other categories as well. A person that stands up straight with their shoulders back will be perceived as more confident and "powerful" than someone who's hunching over and looking at the ground. These are just a few small examples, the art of body language can do much more than help you sell something to a client or be perceived better. Some studies have shown that 60% of our communication is actually non verbal, so mastering body language may be more valuable to you than mastering the art of talking. I'll give you one last example. Two guys approach the same girl, both wanting to get her number. The first one delivers the most epic pick-up line, however he's hunching over, shaking and looking at the ground. The second guy, says something completely boring (ex. "Hey, where's the nearest Starbucks?"), however he's smiling, staying straight and looks confident. The girl will most probably freak out when she hears the first one and walk away, while the second guy has a great chance of the conversation going on and him getting her number.

All in all, knowing how to use your body properly may help you in many areas in your life (from your career to your relationship), and knowing how to understand what other people feel through body language can also help you connect with them or make them do something for you (like selling them a product).

Appearance

The first of the four body language sections will be about **appearance**. Although, technically this isn't really body language, we still decided to include it as such because it wasn't relevant enough to have its own chapter.

In this part, we will mainly be focused on **clothing, grooming and accessories,** as they all convey different status symbols and emotions. Let me give you a quick example - When you see a person that wears a tailored suit along with a luxurious watch, you immediately assume that the person is responsible, wealthy, confident and many other positive characteristics. However, that person may not be the wealthy businessman that you think they are. They may be a regular person who just knows how to dress well and which clothes are best suited for which occasion. So, if your goal is to look rich without being rich, simply go out and buy a well tailored suit, a watch that looks like a Rolex and a great pair of shoes, and you'll be set. Keep in mind that overdoing this may lead to a negative effect (making you look less rich than you actually are), so stay away from really flashy clothes, keep it neat and simple.

We discussed how you can end up looking rich without being rich, but that may not be your goal. Maybe your goal is to look more ambitious, confident, calm, punctual etc? The same look that we described before can bring you the illusion of these personality traits as well. But, what if suits aren't your cup of tea? Well then, you can opt for subtler options, such as: dress shirts, chinos, quality sunshades, along with some other formal outfits.

Now that I explained what wearing a suit makes other people think about you, it's time to explore some other clothing options. If your goal is to look like a chill, cool and interesting guy/girl, wearing some casual clothes may be the best option. I'd probably advise you to wear a pair of skinny jeans (not super skinny if you are a dude), along with an oversized hoodie/t-shirt. As for shoes, you can opt for any type of sneakers (just try to avoid really flashy or sporty models). You may also want to add a few accessories such as watches, necklaces, rings etc. And also, if you live in a cooler area, you'll need to add a third layer to your top outfit (bomber jackets work great) and choose a great pair of boots. This may be a very basic look, but it's a great starting point if you're new to fashion. As you continue building your wardrobe, you should start looking at other options, such as streetwear.

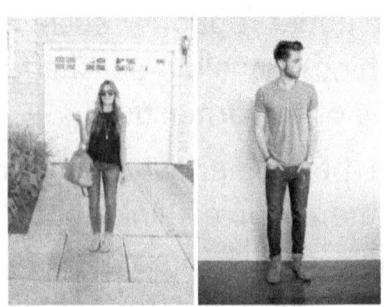

Okay so, now you know what you should be wearing, but what about the clothes that you should avoid? I'd say you should always avoid clothes that don't fit you well, as they'll just point out the bad features of you body (make you look shorter, skinnier or plumpier). The next thing you want to avoid is clothes that are dirty and un-ironed. Unless your goal is to go along with street gangs, i'd say you avoid dirty and worn off clothing.

All in all, this chapter gives you a great starting point with becoming a better person and being taken more seriously. It may also help understand that people may not actually be what they look like (ex. - A guy in a suit may not be rich, but he gives the illusion that he has a ton of money).

Posture

The second section of this chapter will be about posture. You've been told to stand and sit straight since you were a little child. Your parents would always pat you on the back when you would slouch, telling you that it's very unhealthy. And yeah, it is unhealthy. It may cause many diseases and deformities such as scoliosis and lordosis. However, having good posture may have other benefits that aren't related to health.

Mainly speaking, having good posture will help you increase your confidence and make you look like a better person. For example, hunching over and looking to the ground while speaking to co-workers or clients will make you look insecure and scared. Once you start standing straight, they'll start taking you more seriously, which means that you'll have a better overall career. It may sound impossible that a simple thing like having good posture can help you make more money, but it's true. If don't believe me, just ask yourself. Would you rather trust a salesman that's well dressed (previous chapter), stands straight and looks you in the eyes while talking, or a salesman that's looking at the ground and has his shoulders hunched over? The answer is pretty clear.

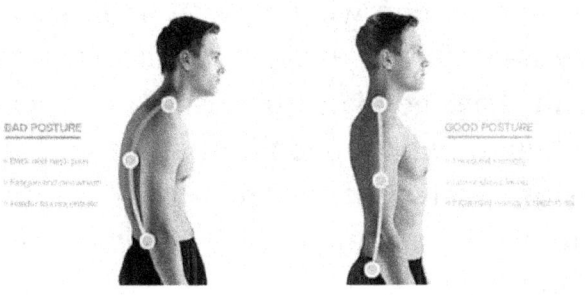

Although, making more money is great, there's something even better that good posture can bring you - more love. At first, this may sound stupid and naive, but let me explain myself. If you want to start a great relationship, you need to approach members of the opposite sex (or same sex, depending on what you're into). Once you approach them, the first impression is the most crucial part of your interaction. If you come up to a girl and start a conversation while looking at the ground and hunching over, she'll probably see you as an unattractive option. Having the best pick-up lines doesn't really matter if your body language conveys that you are an insecure person. It doesn't really matter what you say, all that matters is how you say it.

This information will help you understand how people feel. People that are straight up and have good posture usually feel very confident, while people that have bad posture feel insecure and shy. This may help you analyze people's feelings and intentions.

Know that you know the benefits and meanings of posture, it's time to teach you how to get a good one yourself. I suggest you start with by standing up, and carrying your weight on the balls of your feet. Next, you should bend your knees slightly. Make sure your legs are shoulder width apart. Relax your arms, and let them hang naturally. Stand straight, and pull your shoulders back. Lastly, you'd want to tuck in your stomach. This simple guide will not only improve your health and remove any pain you have in your back, it'll also make you look a lot more confident and be taken a lot more seriously. Additionally, I need to note that if you are diagnosed with a back problem or you think that you have one, you should always consult your doctor first.

In conclusion, having good posture means being confident, while having bad posture means the opposite. Make sure to follow the simple guide and make yourself look like a stud.

Physical Movement

This section will be focused on analyzing other people's body language, rather than using your own body language to come off as a more confident person. Understanding how different moves have different meanings can help you better understand your clients, potential mates or every day people. I'll discuss a few different movements and tell you what their meaning is.

First, we start with **leaning in** (or out). This one is used by women quite often. Usually when they're talking to a guy that's trying to attract them. If you're talking to a girl, and she starts leaning in towards you, it means that she's interested in what you're saying and that she may be attracted to you. However, if she's doing the opposite (leaning back), she may not feel comfortable around you. A good way to check if she's interested is actually leaning in towards her. If she moves back or looks at you weirdly, it's a red flag and you should step back. However if she's leans back as well, it's a sign that you should go on and plan your next move.

Second, we have - **distance**. Distance is a crucial part of any conversation. If someone is moving away from you while you're talking the person may feel intimidated, unsafe or uncomfortable around you. If they're coming close to you on the other hand, it's a sign that they're attracted to you or simply like you as a person. If you notice that people are constantly walking away when you spark a conversation, you may be too hostile in your approaches. Try calming down a bit and taking things a bit less seriously.

The next movement that I'll discuss is **crossing your arms**. This one is also widely used by women when they feel unsafe and try to tell a man that they aren't attracted to them. Basically, if you're talking to a girl and she moves away while crossing her arms, it's a sign that you're either too fast, or she's simply not attracted to you. On the contrary, she may have her arms open and moving. This is a signal that she's having fun and that she's interested in you.

Now, we go on to **lip biting**. Lip biting can signal a few different emotions and intentions. For example, if you're talking to a girl and she shows the other signs of interest (previous three) and she's also biting her lips, it means that she's preparing them for a kiss. So, if you're wondering if you should kiss her, just look at her lips. One other meaning of lip biting is nervousness. People who are nervous and insecure around others usually shows signs such as lip biting, nail biting, fidgeting and even blushing.

Next, we have **playing with hair.** If you're having a conversation with a girl, and she's constantly playing with her hair and twitching it between her fingers, it may mean that she's attracted to you, but also shy (thus the nervousness).

All in all, understanding how physical movements in a conversation convey different emotions can help you comprehend what people are feeling and what their intentions are.

Facial Expressions

We covered every single part of the human body (from posture to arm movement), yet we didn't mention the most important one - the face. As with all the other body parts, facial expressions can convey different emotions and intentions. These are a bit easier to understand as most of you probably know the meaning of a few (if not all) facial expressions. Below you'll find a list of the most common facial expressions and their meaning.

Anger. When a person is angry at something (or someone), they usually flex their eyebrows and bring them down. They also seem to open their eyes to the max. The person's forehead is also flexed, as well as the mouth.

Happiness. When a person is happy they show a bright smile and uncover their teeth. They also bring their eyebrows up. They say that smiling and being happy uses much less muscles than being angry and frowning, so if your goal is to avoid wrinkles, make sure to use this expressions as much as possible.

Surprise. We've all been here, it's your birthday, and you come home to a giant party organized by your family. You open up your mouth and eyes to the max. You also bring your forehead along with your eyebrows up.

Fear. When someone's afraid of something, they may try to hide it to avoid critics. However, once the fear becomes too big to carry, they usually express it in many ways, one of which is their face. They open up their mouth slightly while bringing the inner side of their eyebrows up. Their forehead is also flexed and brought up.

Disgust. Imagine this - You're having lunch at the nearest mall, and suddenly you feel the urge to use the bathroom. You go to the mall restroom, and guess what, it's as disgusting as it usually is. You flex your forehead and cheeks, making them almost covering your eyes. You also close your mouth and bring it up.

Sadness. This one is the one that you'd like to see the least, nevertheless, it's still present in many people's lives. When someone is sad, they usually bring their mouth down (do an inverted smile, while relaxing their forehead and bringing their eyebrows down.

Neutrality. Sometimes, a person's face may not show any of these signs, does this mean they're emotionless? No. They're simply feeling neutral at the moment and have nothing going on in their brain. A neutral expression has all the muscles relaxed.

These 7 facial expressions are the ones that you'll be meeting all the time, however, there are other less common and relevant expressions which you'll be able to understand when you're more experienced with analyzing people. These 7 are a great place to start. Below you'll see an image that shows each expression in real life.

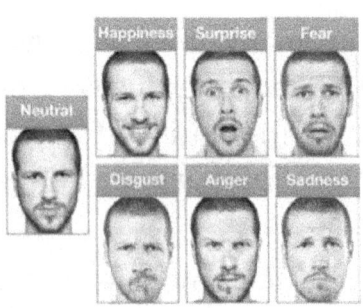

Chapter 20: The Art of Flirting

Flirting is an age -old tradition as well as being a normal human impulse. We have to figure out how to get along with members of the opposite sex (or same, if that's your preference) so we figure out how to attract their attention. Flirting is not just a "courtship ritual", it is also a survival instinct and a necessary component of any healthy relationship.

According to the Merrium -Webster, "Flirt" is defined as one behaving as though attracted to or trying to attract someone, but for amusement rather than with serious intentions."

So basically, flirting is acting silly and showing interest in someone simply because it's fun. But that definition isn't entirely true...

...Because people flirt with serious intent all the time. Why?

It's an exciting and low-risk method of starting a conversation with someone you're attracted to. And it works. Flirting is lighthearted chatting that involves teasing, physical touching, cracking jokes, giving compliments, and being slightly absurd but not weird.

People flirt when they're attracted to someone but don't want to come out and say it right away (which is smart because doing so might scare off a potential mate.)

Flirting is a delicate art that takes practice and confidence, and if done correctly, will make talking to every girl infinitely easier. It can bring two people closer together and also be very sexy. It is important that you recognise when you are being flirted with, otherwise you may possibly miss out on a potential date. And that's why we're going to show you how to do it.

Importance Of Flirting

When carried out in the correct manner, flirting can be the initial reason for two people becoming close. The main purpose of flirting is to send out signals to others that you are attracted to them and would like to get to know them. It is just as important for you to learn how to flirt accurately and appropriately as it is for you to recognise when you are being flirted with. By not recognising flirting signs, you risk missing a flirting opportunity which could have resulted in you meeting a very special person.

Flirting Signs

Flirting occurs in a variety of forms, some being more obvious than others. In general flirting signs are similar for both men and women; however there are some flirting signs unique to women. Often a man will not even realise he is being flirted with, unless a woman gives a clear sign, but many flirting signs are more subtle. Flirting plays a key role in finding a potential date that could lead to a successful relationship, therefore the importance of recognising flirting signs cannot be underestimated. Many flirting signs are carried out unintentionally, but whether it is intentional or not, it could still be the reason for you meeting someone special.

Forms of flirting includes facial expression, body language and even the way someone speaks. These are known as flirting signs. Some flirting signs arequite obvious, such as winking, smiling, gazing, the raising of eye brows and gentle touching on the arm. Other flirting signs aren't so obvious, for example, having dilated pupils, copying of body movements, copying tone of voice and even sitting up straight. Which ever flirting signs you choose to use, be careful not to overuse them.

1. Facial Expression

A facial expression is one of the most obvious flirting signs to express. Most guys who want to get good with girls focus primarily what to say when they first start out. Pretty early on, it's good you focus on facial expressions. Explained below are look at seven of the best facial expression to ramp up your sex appeal with women.

–The Cute And Sexy Look

This one's something of a "bread and butter" look for interacting with women - it automatically slots you into "sexy guy" territory, and you'll want to do it as much as possible... perhaps even turn it into your default facial expression. The cute and sexy look really ramps up interest from women, and causes them to view you as a curious, interesting, sexual man and one very much worth getting to know.

This look is effective at placing you firmly into the 'lover' category removing much of the risk of ending up in the friend zone or as an early boyfriend candidate. That's because more platonic men simply don't use it, and if you do, she knows automatically which category you go in (the bold, naughty, sexy man).

It isn't going to pick girls up for you, of course you've still got to do that yourself. But if you want to have an easier time of it with everything you do with women, this look contributes to that quite strongly. Test it out, if you haven't already you'll almost certainly find it useful.

– The Value-Giving Smile

You may begin to ask yourself what does a "value-giving" smile mean?

By this I mean someone tells a joke or makes a witty comment, and you want to smile/laugh a little bit, in a high status way. The communication here is, "All right, I'll give you that one! That's funny."

Or s omeone tells a story about something he or she did that is cool, different, or exciting, and you want to show them a little admiration without oozing it. Here the communication is, "Well, you don't say! That's neat."

Or y ou see someone you haven't seen in a while (although it's fine to use on dates too, assuming the girl isn't overly serious), and want to show them you're happy to see them in a high status way without having to use words, get up, be overly expressive, etc. In this case, the communication is, "Hey, it's you! Great to see you again, old friend."

You'll notice the characteristics of this one are genuine smile, with eyes crinkled at the corners (fake smiles don't have this eye-corner crinkling; genuine smiles do). Reasonably broad smile, though broader on one side of the mouth than the other. Some teeth showing, but not a fully open-mouth smile; this smile's a mix of the sexy smile and the warm, friendly one. Eyebrows slightly pulled up, almost imperceptibly so

Often accompanied with a slight, slow head tilt backwards (not dramatic or significant; slight), followed by a nod forward to return the head to its original position, with a bit of "bounce" as the head settles into place

This expression is great for conveying feelings of warmth and familiarity; the instant you do this with someone, they feel as though the two of you are old friends... even if it's only your first date, or you've only just met her and you're acknowledging her as she returns from the bathroom.

— The Sexy Pouty LookIf you thought only little girls and sultry grown up minxes pouted, think again.

The sexy pouty look is often the domain of younger men, simply because it's a more "tormented" look... and younger men tend to be the more tormented, angstier men (older men just tend to have their stuff together, and don't need / use the pouty look all that often... although you can still find Brad Pitt and Sylvester Stallone using itquite a bit, even as they grow longer in tooth).

This expression is fairly similar to the cute and sexy look, except that it lacks the latter's hints of playfulness.

The features sexy pouty has in common with cute and sexy are the slightly pursed lips, eyebrows either up or down, though not as exaggeratedly as in cute and sexy, an underlook, and with chin tucked down and eyes looking up.

Some of the differences include no hint of playfulness in lips, and no slight smile, eyes sad and unfocused; looking slightly down (as opposed to locked onto one's conversation partner with lively incisiveness, as with the cute and sexy look).

Sexy pouty works well when you're going for "young, lost, and vulnerable," and makes you especially likely to get approached by women and opened by them. You appear alluring and vexingly interesting with this look... and also like you won't put up a fight (or turn her down) if she walks up to say 'hello'.

—"Come On... I Know You Want Me" This is one of my favorite facial expressions. For me personally, this one even beats Cute and Sexy.

"Come On... I Know You Want Me" is what you give to girls when they resist you, when they try to act like they're not interested in you, when they're trying to play coy, when they're trying to wind down the sexual energy, and when they're trying to friend zone you or throw you in the boyfriend box.

It's a great way of telling the girl, "Nice try, but I'm not falling for it. You want me." Which is good for lightening the mood a bit... while at the same time, kicking the sexual tension up another notch.

While doing this kind of facial expression, you've got to be somewhat cocksure to pull it off... you've really got to think you're some hot stuff.

However, when you DO think this... and you communicate it with this expression... very often, the women you use it with are inclined to think the same.

R emember to use these facial expressions in moderation. Simply pick out the ones you would feel most comfortable using and practice them. It may help to look in a mirror and observe yourself, even if it makes you feel a little silly. Without a doubt the most important facial expression is a smile. Not only does a smile show that you are a friendly person, it also shows that you are approachable which is highly important when flirting.

2. Body movement

Male flirting body language is usually not so rich. Normally, men display signals that display power, wealth and status and are not very good at sending or receiving signals used in courtship game; mostly they simply react to what they see. As a man, you can straighten your tie, touch your watch, and brush imaginary dust of your shoulder.

The most aggressive signals of male flirting body language, include thumbs - in-belt gestures that convey authority, confidence and draws attention to his crotch area. You may also turn hyour body towards her, and point your foot towards her. On top of this, you may hold her gaze longer than it feels comfortable. If you are sitting down, you may also spread your legs to emphasize your crotch. In fact, you may adjust your crotch right there in public – an attempt to assert your masculinity in front of the woman you desire.

Whether you are standing or sitting it is important to keep your posture as tall as possible. Not only will this make you feel more confident, it will also make you look more confident, plus help to show off your manly figure.

As with the facial expressions, it is important not to overuse these flirting signs otherwise you risk giving off the wrong impression or appear anxious and uncomfortable. Select a handful of these body movements which you feel most comfortable using and stick to them. You may find you carry out some of these body movements without even realising, don't worry about this, if you don't even realise it then it is natural for you to do so.

laugh at things she says

This is in no way a slight on your comedic timing, which we're sure is spectacular. No matter how funny you are, the person who likes you is always going to find you about 10x as humorous as the person who doesn't.

You've probably experienced this yourself. Do you find yourself giggling at even the mildest joke that your crush offers? We can't help eating up everything that person says. Remember this tendency when you notice a guy grinning and chuckling at everything you say.

Try to make her laugh

In the same vein, we are instinctively drawn to people who are funny. Who doesn't want to spend the majority of their day upbeat and laughing about something? As a guy, you need to know that a sense of humor rates highly on a girl's "boyfriend wish list."

P ay attention to her positive reaction to a bit and then bring up something similar repeatedly. In addition to trying to make her smile, this helps to establish inside jokes.

3. Remember the little things

Remembering the small details about a person's life takes sincere effort. We all have enough going on that we don't go around making this effort with others unless we genuinely care about the person.

This could manifest itself in a variety of discrete but thoughtful ways. If she mentions an upcoming event to you, such as her birthday, you should ask her how it went the next time you see her. You could also pay attention to her favorite drink order and have it ready for her next time you meet. When you show a girl that you're filled with details about her, she'll show her hand.

Flirting Do's And Don'ts

Getting flirting right cannot be underestimated. Take on board these "do's" and "don'ts" of flirting to make sure you don't make those common flirting mistakes.

Flirting - Do's

The more these techniques are practiced, the more natural they will become to you, resulting in you appearing confident and enjoying yourself.

— Make sure you have a smile on your face. This will show that you are a kind happy person enjoying yourself. A smile is often the first flirting sign a potential date would notice, so a warm smile could attract someone to you.

— Give compliments to the person you are flirting with. Compliments are a good way to make someone feel special and good about themselves.

— When flirting, make sure you have regular eye contact with the person you are flirting with. Try to make it look natural remembering not to stare otherwise you might scare them off.

— When having a conversation stick to topics you enjoy and are interested in. This will help to keep conversation flowing plus show that you are an interesting happy person.

— Try to ask questions to the person you are flirting with. This will show that you are genuinely interested in them. This is a good idea especially if you have been introduced by a friend as it can help to break the ice.

— Listen carefully to what the other person is saying. By showing an interest in them you are showing that you are considerate and genuinely enjoy their company.

—Casually touch the person you are flirting with on the arm or hand to show that you are interested in them but be careful not to overdo it.

— Make sure you sit up straight with your chin held high. Sitting or standing tall gives you the confidence you need for perfect flirting moments.

— Always offer your hand to shake if introduced by a friend. This automatically informs the other person that you are genuinely pleased to meet them. Use this opportunity to see how long your hand is held for. A warm handshake may set the flirting moment off to an excellent start.

— When starting a discussion, try to use phrases such as "I think" or "I wonder". By starting a sentence this way you are leaving the discussion open for the other person to share their opinion.

As you practice these techni ques, you will become an expert at flirting without overdoing it. You will also learn how to relax and really enjoy yourself.

Flirting - Don'ts

Getting flirting wrong is unfortunately very easy. With the intention of attracting someone, you could actually find yourself scaring them away before you have even said a word. You want to give the impression that you are genuine and want to get to know them, not to come across as being uninterested or only after a physical relationship. If you avoid the following classic flirting disasters at all costs, you will have many successful flirting moments.

—It is crucial that you avoid tasteless chat-up lines. Chat-up lines instantly put people off and are a major catastrophe for flirting.

— Try not to fidget. Fidgeting shows that you are nervous and uncomfortable, which are not characteristics you want to show your flirting partner.

— Make an effort not to look down to the ground while flirting. Make sure you look at the eyes of the person you are flirting with to show you are keen and paying attention to them. At the same time, remember not to stare at them. You want regular eye contact holding their gaze slightly longer than usual.

—Avoid using phrases such as "y'know" or "yeah". These phrases may make you look uneducated and a possible turn-off for many.

— Don't cross your arms across your chest while flirting. This gives the impression that you are defensive and untrusting towards others, which is not the impression you want to give out when flirting.

— When having a discussion, don't use sounds such as "erm" or "huh". These are sounds that will make you sound anxious and uncomfortable.

— Avoid biting or chewing your nails and picking skin while flirting. These disgusting habits are not for flirting moments. Keep this behaviour for behind closed doors.

Flirting is meant to be an enjoyable experience, not a trauma. By following these simple suggestions, you will learn that flirting is all about having fun and not something to worry about. As you practice these techniques, flirting will become natural to you and you will hopefully find yourself having many successful dates.

Chapter 21: The Four Personality Types

The four personality traits that have commonly been used to distinguish among the temperaments of different people are choleric, sanguine, phlegmatic and melancholic. Hippocrates was among the earliest to describe these four personality types as personality traits and behaviors affected by four bodily fluids. The early Greeks had managed to coin these personality types as temperaments, and they used them to distinguish among people from their character and traits. In the modern world, the four personality types have been used to categorize people accordingly.

Galen was another important philosopher who was responsible for coming up with the personality types by linking them to physical conditions in the world. According to him, the four personality types could be linked to dry/wet and hot/cold situations. These earthly substances were linked to the temperament of a person and used as a basis for coming up with the personality types. Bodily humor played a significant role in determining the four personality types and quickly became associated with everybody. Medical science has progressed since and the personality traits are used by psychologists today to great effect to understand each person and provide an apt diagnosis.

Different aspects of personality are responsible for determining each of the four temperaments. However, it is not unusual for a person to display more than one type of personality trait depending on their mood and what type of activity they are engaged in. There is no standard combination for any of the personality traits as it is impossible to pinpoint to a person's temperaments. Linking each of the personality traits to an element in the world makes it easier to understand the inspiration behind it and the actual personality trait of the person:

Choleric

A choleric personality is one which describes a decisive and independent person who is driven to achieve specific objectives. Such people are usually extroverts and enjoy interacting with others as this is an important aspect of how they socialize. Such people tend to be leaders because they are constantly setting goals for themselves, and they also tend to be outgoing but not shy. This personality trait can be linked to brash leaders who are always at the forefront of attention and looking to provide guidance to everybody else.

One of the major characteristics of this personality type is that the person is usually outgoing and ambitious in their nature. Such people are always looking to discover and lead by example, and it is very difficult not to notice them in society because they make an effort to be seen. This personality type is linked to fire as a comparison to one of the elements in the world, and this signifies the ability of the person to rule over others. People who have this personality trait also like having a fact-based opinion of the world. They are also very straightforward in their views.

A good example of a choleric personality type is a leader such as Donald Trump who enjoys being at the head of any social and professional group he is involved in. He is very goal-oriented and will pursue his interests with intense vigor while at the same time emphasizing his leadership skills and the need for everybody to support him. Trump is a typical choleric leader because he also looks at the world from a fact-based approach and it is not easy to convince him otherwise. His personality trait also characterizes decisiveness as well as ambition as he has come to be known throughout the country.

Sanguine

A sanguine personality is described as one that is very active, social, and enthusiastic. A person with this personality type is easy to talk to because they enjoy it, and they are never satisfied with doing nothing. It is quite difficult to find such a person seated by themselves without anything to do because they are always all over the place. The noisemaker of the classroom tends to be sanguine because they are rarely calm and 'to themselves'. They enjoy interacting with others greatly, and they can be 'the life of the party' because their liveliness can be infectious.

The talkative nature of such people is an important characteristic that marks out a sanguine personality. They enjoy being part of a crowd, and they are very social people who are easy to approach and interact with. Sanguine personalities tend to be charismatic, and this can explain why several people like this specific personality type. Similarly, this personality type describes an extrovert who is more likely to be at a social gathering than at home alone. The earth element linked to this personality type is air, and it signifies the social usefulness of the person.

An example of a character that can be linked to this personality trait would be a celebrity like Justin Bieber. A person such as this would enjoy the company of others and even be a daredevil when in the company of friends. Such a person enjoys risky activity and will probably engage in a risky activity faster than they will have time to think about it. Such a person would enjoy performing at parties and generally hanging out with everybody and getting to know every single individual at the event.

Phlegmatic

This personality type differs significantly from the first two as it describes a person who is relaxed, peaceful and quiet. Such people are more composed and would prefer their own company rather than hanging out at a noisy place with lots of people. A phlegmatic individual tends to be easygoing, and it would probably be interesting to interact with such a person because it would be a very calm and relaxed interaction. Such people would prefer to stay away from trouble, and they are known for generalizing their thoughts and opinions on most matters.

Some of the major characteristics of individuals who possess phlegmatic personality traits are that they tend to hide their emotions and keep to themselves. It is difficult to know what is going on in the head of a phlegmatic individual because they do not speak much and would rather conceal their feelings. However, they are sympathetic individuals who display typical characteristics of introverts and are well known for making compromises. Such people tend to be very caring and openly receptive to other people. The element linked to this personality trait is water, and it describes a person who usually focuses on getting what they want in a reserved manner.

A good example of a person displaying this trait would be a primary school teacher. Most of these individuals tend to be sympathetic and understanding, particularly of young ones, and they spend a lot of time helping out their students to be better people. Classroom teachers sometimes do not speak much and only do so when the situation is absolutely necessary. The classroom teacher will be open to engaging with their students but only as much as they can assist them appropriately. They will not be overly outgoing, but they will be receptive enough, particularly to the students and open for interaction.

Melancholic

People who feel very deeply, and think in the same manner, display melancholic personalities. They are even quieter and reserved than phlegmatic people, and they tend to spend a lot of time by themselves lost in their own little worlds. They have very active brains, and they are known to be very creative because they spend a lot of time thinking. Individuals who possess this personality type are very analytical and take everything with the seriousness it deserves; they like details and would likely understand absolutely everything about the things that surround them.

Some of the major characteristics of this personality type include self-reliance and reservation that makes them unique from the rest of the population. It is not usually easy to spot a melancholic individual because they tend to avoid being singled out in a crowd, even if it means awkwardly mingling with those around them. As a classic introvert personality type, melancholic people tend to strive for perfection, and this usually results in them being very organized. The element that represents this trait is earth, and it signifies somebody who avoids too much interaction with the rest of the group.

A good example of individuals who display this character trait would be book authors such as Stephen King. They tend to be thinkers who spend a lot of time to themselves and are constantly organizing their thoughts to come up with different deals. Stephen King is a person very much reserved to himself and enjoys the time he spends alone as it offers him an opportunity to think of new book ideas. Stephen King is less likely to attend a party and more likely to be very tidy and detailed because his profession demands this of him.

Understanding the different personality types is instrumental in ensuring that you master the social skills necessary for interacting with everybody else. Comprehending the different personality types makes it even easier to analyze people from their body language and facial expressions. It becomes possible to make accurate judgments about somebody's character and preferences, thereby minimizing the chances of making mistakes when interacting with the individual. A key part of developing your social skills is learning to differentiate between the different personality types as it allows you to understand the manner of interaction to engage with each person.

CHAPTER 22: WHAT IS EMOTIONAL INTELLIGENCE?

It is almost certain that you have heard of emotional quotient, EQ, and emotional intelligence before, but have you ever asked yourself if you are emotionally intelligent? To go one step further, are you emotionally intelligent at work? What about as a leader?

If you have pondered these questions, you may have also asked yourself why emotional intelligence is so important. In this chapter, I will share more about emotional intelligence and its importance to every person, every workplace, every society, and even to the entire world.

What is emotional intelligence?

According to psychologists Peter Salovey and John Mayer, emotional intelligence is "the ability to perceive emotions, to access and generate emotions, to understand emotions and emotional knowledge, and to reflectively regulate emotions so as to promote emotional and intellectual growth."

In layman's terms, it is the extent to which we are self-aware (able to recognize and understand our emotions), can self-manage (able to adapt and control our emotions and reactions), can motivate ourselves (taking the right actions to achieve a goal), can express empathy for other people, and possess strong social skills (ability to build positive relationships with others).

Emotional intelligence is measured through standardized tests and the result of these tests is called the Emotional Quotient (EQ). The higher your EQ is, the better. However, unlike the Intelligence Quotient (IQ), which is often fixed by the time you reach a certain age, most scholars and psychologists believe that EQ is malleable and can be enhanced and learned.

EQ may not be as well-known as IQ, yet many experts deem it as more important than IQ. Why? Studies show EQ is a better predictor of success, quality of relationships, and happiness of a person. It is evident everywhere and is critical in all aspects of life.

Have you ever heard someone make statements like these: "Wow, what a positive person. He will surely achieve something great in life." or "She is very caring and sociable. She is such a great boss."

These comments illustrate that when a person has high EQ (even when the person does not know it), it is seen and felt by others. It is these types of individuals that others tend to believe will most likely attain success. So, why is EQ important to everyone?

1. EQ is absolutely an important part of forming, developing, maintaining, and enhancing personal relationships with others. It is undeniable that people who know how to build positive relationships with other people will most likely be successful in their fields.

Workers with high EQ can work harmoniously in teams and adjust to changes. No matter how intelligent you are, if you have low emotional intelligence, you may find the path to success a struggle. However, there is good news. Take comfort in knowing that you can improve your EQ skills at any age and regardless of past behavior.

2. Being aware of oneself means being able to handle constructive criticisms. You would probably agree that there is no perfect person in the world and in everything we do, we need other people's criticisms and communication to do better.

If you have a high EQ, you are self-aware, meaning you understand your strengths, admit your weaknesses, and understand how your actions will affect other people surrounding you.

Your high EQ allows you to take these criticisms as an opportunity to improve your performance. This is a crucial part of working in an environment with many stakeholders.

3. Self-motivated people can inspire everyone. When a person is self-

motivated, others around them often evaluate their own level of motivation. A self-motivated person is optimistic and is driven by what really matters to him/her.

Who would not want a self-motivated person around, right? Motivation is contagious and a highly-motivated household, workplace, or society will repeatedly outperform non-motivated ones. Low-motivation may be a sign that your emotional quotient is low in one or more of the key EQ quadrants.

4. EQ makes the world genuine. People with a high Emotional Quotient have compassion that allows them to connect with others on an "emotional level." If a person is able to empathize with others, then he/she will work genuinely and attend to others' needs with compassion and care; even during times of challenge.

5. Having a high EQ means being able to control yourself in all situations. Your fellow employee shouts at you angrily for some unknown reason. Given this scenario, would you be able to control

your emotions and not act the same way he did?

You see, EQ is connected to how we control both our positive and our negative emotions. Think back to some of the decisions in your life you are not proud of. Ask yourself how many of them related to a lack of self-control or a lack of impulse control? The answer may be surprising.

Do you have greater clarity around what emotional intelligence and emotional quotient are? Do you agree that it is more important than being "book-intelligent" or having a high IQ? Can you see why EQ is the key to success?

I refer to emotional intelligence as the missing link. You know it when you see it... even if you cannot identify it. The challenge is when emotional intelligence is missing it is not always easy to identify. It is often clear that a problem exists but exactly what the problem is may be a mystery.

Knowing what you know about emotional intelligence I have a challenge for you. Ask yourself this question: are you an emotionally intelligent person at home and at work? If the answer is yes, you are on the right track. Continue along this path, strengthening your EQ skills as you go, and you could be well on your way to success. If your answer is no, do not worry.

Emotional intelligence is a set of skills you can improve with focus and a sound strategy. Regardless of where you are today, you cannot go wrong investing in yourself and improving your emotional intelligence skills.

Chapter 23: Significance of your verbal and non-verbal cues

To start with, let us first understand the significance of our verbal and non-verbal cues. The way we express ourselves verbally allows us to explain and get our point across or at least that is what we think. The reality may be that you are giving off a very different message if your body does not offer expressions to back up what you are saying.

Let us take a very simple example. You may feel scared of something, say a dog.However, you may not want to admit it. The truth is your body language is most likely to give away exactly how you feel. As you approach the dog, you may start trembling or you may not bring yourself to touch the dog with ease. It becomes pretty evident that you are scared in such a case without you having to admit it.

Let us take another example. You may see a young couple nearby. How are you able to determine that they are actually a couple in a relationship? Sometimes you do not need to be told. It is pretty evident on its own with the body language of people. The way they may look at each other, the way they talk to each other, their gestures etc. are all indications that give away the status of their relationship.

What are the non-verbal cues?

In the simplest form, non-verbal cues are the way you express yourself in any other way apart from the verbal responses. More commonly, it is stated as the body language. So what are the different forms of body language?

Facial Expressions. Our face especially our eyes are an outlet for expression. As they say, what we feel inside is evident on the outside. In most cases, this rings true. If we are happy, our facial expressions allow us to express it by smiling. If we smile genuinely, it is evident from our eyes. As they say, our eyes cannot lie. It becomes evident to those who are able to analyze these cues well.

Body Posture. This is another way to analyze the true act of expression. You can determine from a person's gait and his posture if he/she is confident, arrogant, shy, conscious etc.

Body gestures. These vary from person to person. A person may start twitching when he/she is nervous, tremble when scared, play with their fingers, move their legs restlessly while sitting, play with their hair, bite on their lips, have a distant look in their eyes, get restless, watery eyed etc.

Why do our verbal and non-verbal cues differ at times?

The truth is that society molds us into what we are expected to be and not what we want to be ourselves. Situations, experiences and circumstances change people and make them act as though this is who they really are. In the midst of this, one can tend to forget who they really are. How is that? It is a fact that throughout our lives, we are faced with different pressures with the expectation to not ask questions and just get on with things.

These expectations may be from your parents, siblings, spouse, friends, colleague and peers. Hence, without knowing it, we are always under some sort of pressure. This molds us into becoming a different kind of person. It is also true that all of us lie to ourselves to one extent or the other. This may be intentional or unintentional.

Do not worry if you do not understand all this for now. There is a very deep thought to this. Take a moment and analyze your life. To some extent, you do what others expect you to do, what you are supposed to do as the right option; and other things because you are obligated to do. What if there were no strings attached to anything? What if society had not molded you? Would you behave differently than you do now? It is important to analyze this so as to allow you to understand that we have been affected by pressures around us that include environmental influences.

Why these non-verbal cues are important?

The background that was just given to you was important to determine why our verbal cues differ from our non-verbal cues. We tend to lie to ourselves by not admitting what we are truly feeling at times because of the way we are expected to be. In other cases, people just do not like showing their feelings as they believe it is a sign of weakness. The reasons may vary for different individuals.

Now, why are these non-verbal cues important? I think you can answer this by now. It is so that you can evaluate the true feelings of an individual. If the verbal and non-verbal cues of a person are in synchrony, then the person is displaying his or her true feelings. If not, then you may need to evaluate the body language of a person carefully. This is because we tend to alter our verbal responses but do not focus on our non-verbal cues.

Significance of your body language: Our body language does not only help us to judge the real feelings and intentions of a person but they can also allow us to be more productive in our personal as well as professional lives.

At a personal level, it allows you to get your message across in a better manner and hence strengthens our ability to communicate more effectively. On the other hand, it offers you great productivity at the professional level. How? You are normally analyzed or judged at different job interviews, meetings etc. You are able to give off a stronger profile if you appear more confident which again, is evidenced by your body language.

Let us take an example here. You generally rate your teachers and professors and believe some are better than others. How? Some of them are able to convey the message in a better manner while others are just come across as boring or dull. This is because the overall impact of a person is important. A person may teach well but adopt a monotonous tone, speak in a low voice and appear to lack confidence. Despite his or her abilities, they will struggle to perform well.

On the other hand, a person who speaks in an audible voice, appears confident, uses appropriate body gestures and is able to cover up for his or her flaws; even if they are unable to teach as effectively as the example given previously, will be far more effective. This is because they are able to maintain the attention span of the students and hence deliver the lecture in a more passionate and emotive manner.

Chapter 24: How to deliver a speech and connect to the audience

Steve Jobs: "People, who know what they're talking about, don't need PowerPoint."

In 2005, Steve Jobs, the CEO of Apple, delivered a speech to the University of Stanford. It was actually a commencement address and it remained in history, for being the kind of speech that delivered a powerful message. It was also appreciated for its well-organized structure and quality of delivery.

Speech delivery, a process of simplicity

If you were to look back in time, you would immediately discover that some of the best speeches out there, were the simple ones. They had a clear message to deliver, one that had relevance to the audience, for whom it was intended in the first place. Moreover, the speech was accompanied by stories, these being commonly used to illustrate talking points.

When you are preparing a speech, you might be tempted to spend a lot of time, creating PowerPoint presentations and gathering data to dazzle the audience. However, instead of wasting so much energy and time, it might be for the best to keep things simple. Go for the kind of speech that is clear and relevant at the same time; make sure that it has a simple structure, with introduction, middle and conclusion. Always stick to one theme and do not divagate too much from the subject.

A wise person once said that speeches rarely succeed in communicating useful information, as the speaker most often tries to impress, rather than send a message. Moreover, most people have a short attention span, not to mention memory, so they rarely remember the things said in a speech. If you want to guarantee that your speech is not just noise to the audience, you need to focus on delivering a simple and well-structured speech.

Humor is a great way to connect to the audience, especially if you feel like the atmosphere is a little bit tense and the crowd displeased with your performance. Anecdotes can be used to deliver key messages, as well to present great stories to the audience. However, you have to pay attention to the type of humor you are actually using and always try to determine if your audience responds to it (and in a positive way, of course).

Storytelling, as it was already mentioned, is a key element of any speech. If you include a lot of stories in your speech, you will definitely manage to connect to the audience. This is because you have lived those experiences and you will find it easier to present them to the public. You can recall those stories and tell everyone what happened, without being forced. When the audience will sense that you are genuine, everything will be smooth from there on. Moreover, stories are easily remembered and often transmitted further, to other people.

Why are stories so essential? The answer is simple. A story establishes an emotional connection with the audience. It reaches people on a deep level and it contributes to the release of dopamine at the level of the brain, thus ensuring that the message of the story sticks. The one thing that matters is that you choose stories relevant to the speech and to the audience to whom you are reaching. Always provide relevant content to the public and you will have very little else to worry about.

At the beginning of the speech, you might be tempted to thank everyone. Well, the audience will not be too patient, so you might want to skip this part and jump right to the speech. Use your stories to give an idea about the content of your speech and do not hesitate to resort to effective body language, to argument your ideas and/or opinions.

In delivering your speech, you need to find a level of comfort, which transmits confidence to the audience. If you are nervous and you begin to cross your arms or clutch your hands, you are actually establishing a balance between you and the audience. They will feel your hesitation and lose interest in what you have to say; once such a thing occur, it will incredibly difficult, if not impossible, to regain their attention.

Pay attention to your posture and avoid slouching, as this is a sign that you are not confident enough. Stand up straight and look people right in the eyes, in order to ensure them that you are there for a reason and that is to deliver a speech. Watch out for your speaking style and avoid being either too aggressive or too soft. Strike a balance, articulate your words and make sure to practice your speech over and over again.

Avoid large pauses but use short ones to replace words that should not be presented in a speech, such as "um", "like" or "so" (verbal ticks). Pauses can also be used with the purpose of emphasizing key points or to give the audience, enough time to react to something you have said. Sometimes, a pause made after a joke or an anecdote, will contribute to the comic effect and establish a better connection with the audience.

In a nutshell, you have to work the room, while enjoying the actual experience of giving a speech. Refrain from reading your speech, as this will turn you into a mechanical individual and the audience will be less inclined to hear you. Plus, if you are going to deliver a speech, it can be extremely boring to read it, word for word. If you are not certain of the content, use Q cards with key notes and refer to them, from time to time.

Just because you are in a large room, this does not mean you have to shout to be heard. Use the microphone and speak at a natural volume, watching out for voice pitches as well (high pitches can be extremely disturbing for the audience, especially when heard through a surround system).

Deliver your speech and look people right in the eyes, maintaining eye contact with each individual, for at least one minute. Avoid fidgeting or fumbling with the equipment, as the people in audience will create a negative image about yourself. Do not keep your hands in your pockets, as this is perceived as a sign of overconfidence and contributes to the above-mentioned negative image. Try to be yourself and expose your own views on a certain subject, through your well-structured and yet simple speech.

Food for thought

1) Can you name a famous speech and give three reasons for which it was good?

2) In your own opinion, describe the connection between giving a speech and storytelling.

3) How does the audience form an opinion about the person standing in front of them, delivering a speech?

Chapter 25: Tones of Voice

While it is not body language strictly speaking, tone of voice falls into the same category as being not completely under conscious control and likely to reveal things about the underlying emotional state of a person speaking. A liar's tone of voice when speaking a lie is often strained, more quiet and less relaxed than his norm. (Although it's not body language strictly speaking, one advantage of considering tone of voice is that it's possible to hear it over the phone, while body language is invisible in phone calls.)

There are also clues, as in all cases, arising from disconnect between words and vocal tone. A set of words, or even a single word, may be posed as a statement or as a question. Consider the greeting "hello." When we answer the phone, we use that word as a greeting normally. In that usage, we inflect the word as if it were a question: "Hello?" We are, in effect, inquiring as to who is calling. When we greet someone we know, the same word is used but inflected as a statement: "Hello," with varying degrees of enthusiasm. On the phone, we don't know who the call is coming from (caller ID aside), and so our greeting is as much question as statement; when greeting someone in person, we do know, and so it's inflected as a statement without interrogative.

When someone is stating a lie, he will often inflect words that are grammatically statements into questions, in effect drawing doubt upon them. For example, an employee might explain absence from work in terms of illness, as "I threw up all over the bathroom." If this statement is inflected to resemble a question (e.g. rising in pitch at the end of the sentence), that's a sign the employee is probably making up a story and had some other reason to take the day off.

Now, two cautions are in order here. First, sometimes people will do the same thing when not lying but merely making a statement they're not certain about, turning a statement into a question because, in their mind, it really is a question. But it's usually clear from context when this is happening. In the case of the employee above, naturally he would know without any ambiguity whether he was sick and what his symptoms were. The other caution is that there are some English dialects in which turning statements into questions in terms of vocal tone and inflection is normal; certain sub-dialects of Southern American English do this, as do some dialects from Southern California.

Besides inflecting a statement as if it were a question, the following quirks in regard to tone of voice are all indicators of possible dishonest:

☐ Exaggerated emphasis, making a point of firmly insisting on the truth of something that normally shouldn't be controversial. For example, a husband telling a wife that he came straight home from the work except for a stop at the grocery store for some milk would usually say this offhand, without much emphasis; if in reality he also stopped to bring flowers to his mistress, he might assert that he only stopped for the milk with a peculiar degree of force.

☐ Mumbling or speaking very quickly, making the words hard to understand. In contrast to exaggerated emphasis, sometimes liars will rapidly rush through a lie, as if hoping that the words will be unnoticed. Sometimes the lie will be buried in a list, with the lie itself stated under the breath.

☐ Vocal tone that doesn't match facial expression. A grim tone accompanying a smile, a forceful tone accompanying hesitant body language, can indicate internal conflicts, which, once again, indicate dishonest.

☐ Higher pitch than normal, a "nervous" quality to the tone, slower and choppier speech than the person normally uses, or an increase in the occurrence of slips of the tongue and grammatical errors, all indicate increased nervousness about what is being said and hence a likelihood that a lie is being spoken.

In all cases, it's important to compare the behavior being observed to a baseline. The thing to look for is patterns of speech, tones of voice, or body language that is unusual for the person, more than to an arbitrary "normal" standard.

Chapter 26: Introverts vs. Extroverts

"Extroverts organize their thoughts by talking and gain more energy by seeking outside stimuli. Introverts on the other hand, store information, reflect first, and then speak afterwards. They feel most rested and rejuvenated after they spend time alone, thinking or reading."

Marti Olsen Lany

We hear a lot about how extroverts rule the world, but is that really true?

The truth is that there are a lot of assumptions made about introverts and what makes them tick. And you may be surprised to learn who is an introvert.

Exercise: Reflect on famous people that you think may be introverts. Next, Google famous introverts to see who shows up. Were you right? Are you surprised by any names on the lists?

It is a common assumption that introverts are lacking in confidence and hate public speaking. While some may fit this profile, this is a broad generalization that is far from true. Conversely, some think that people who are confident when speaking in public must be extroverts. This is not necessarily so.

Have a look at the following summary of the characteristics of introverts and extroverts.

Characteristics of introverts:

Restore their energy with time alone

Prefer smaller gatherings

Find large gatherings exhausting

Get overwhelmed in noisy settings with multiple conversations going on

Internal thinkers

Need time to reflect to generate ideas and to do their best work

Tend not to like change

Characteristics of extroverts:

Restore their energy by being around people

Enjoy large gatherings

Find small gatherings boring

Get into the spirit of meeting people, especially at a big event

Are the only ones who will say, "The more the merrier!"

Think out loud by talking

Come up with ideas seemingly instantly, on the spot

Love change

As you can see, a key difference between introverts and extroverts is how they restore their energy.

Exercise: The next time you attend any conference or other big event, observe what happens when the formal sessions are over. Look in the bar and you will find the extroverts, restoring their energy by talking with other people. The introverts, for the most part, will be in their rooms, or out for a walk, restoring their energy by spending time alone.

Consider these common myths about introverts:

Introverts are shy: It is an assumption that someone who is not talking is shy when, in fact, they may be deep in thought, reflecting on the subject at hand.

Introverts don't have anything to contribute: Just because someone doesn't immediately jump into a conversation doesn't mean they have nothing to say. Perhaps they are inclined to wait until asked, or for a pause before they speak up (which may never happen) or need time to reflect.

Introverts have social anxiety: Maybe yes or maybe no. While it is not uncommon for an introvert to experience social anxiety, not all do, and the degree certainly varies by person and situation.

You may be asking yourself, is introversion a bad thing? No, absolutely not. It is just one of the ways in which humans are different. We will look at other ways people differ in the next chapter. We are simply calling out introversion first, as this book is written to benefit introverts by offering conversation strategies specific to their unique needs.

As we wrap up this chapter, here are a few helpful caveats to keep in mind:

While our society seemingly places a high value on extroverts, keep in mind that introverts contribute just as much to the world, if not more.

Neither introversion nor extroversion is inherently right or wrong–these are just two different ways of being in the world.

Learn to value what makes you tick as an introvert and carve out time to do what you need to do to take care of yourself. If that means you need half an hour of silence to restore your energy while your extrovert co-workers are at the bar, that's fine.

Trust your gut.

Focus on your strengths and build on them.

What do you think? Are you an introvert?

Introversion vs. Extroversion Self-Assessment

Take a few minutes to reflect on whether you are an introvert or an extrovert.

What restores your energy:

a) being with people

b)time alone

What do you prefer:

a)a big party

b)a quiet dinner with a friend

How do you do your best thinking:

a)out loud

b)internally

How do you problem solve:

a)verbally (sharing possibilities with others)

b)internally (reflecting on possibilities as you refine them)

Do your best ideas:

a)come to you right away

b)come to you after you have had time to reflect

If you are at a gathering with multiple conversations going on at the same time, are you:

a)energized by the buzz

b)overwhelmed by the noise

If you are attending a conference, do you tend to:

a) mingle with and meet lots of people

b) keep to yourself

What best describes your ability to concentrate? Are you:

a) easily distracted

b) able to concentrate for long stretches of time

Do you share personal information about yourself with:

a) just about anyone

b) just close family and friends

What best describes how you feel about change. Do you:

a) love it

b) resist it

If you answered the first option (a) more than the second option (b), you are probably an extrovert. That's ok. While this book isn't written specifically for you, you'll probably find you still get plenty of ideas from it.

If you answered the second option (b) more than the first option (a), you are probably an introvert. Great, this book is written for you!

Case Studies

Rebecca never really thought of herself as an introvert, but that changed after she learned that introverts need time alone to restore their energy. That'd be her!

Larry has always thought of himself as outgoing, but supposes he is an introvert because he likes lots of time alone and is very analytic.

Chris knows she is definitely an introvert. There's no hiding it!

Kelly knows he is an extrovert and he is ok with that.

Conclusion

Thanks again for taking the time to download this book!

You should now have a good understanding of where to begin when it comes to learning how to analyze people, and be able to use the rules and suggestions outlined in this book to start your own journey of self-discovery. Analyzing others is not simply about breaking them down into their individual components and reading between the lines, it's also about understanding yourself and how you are perceived in the world. Analyzing people is not just about body language or how someone sounds when they are saying something, it is also about getting rid of your own personal biases and emotions in the moment, and practically looking at things from a structural perspective.

The suggestions at the end of each chapter are geared towards helping beginners not only learn the labels and rules they need to learn, but to also help them in implementing them during real-life encounters. Do not put yourself on the spot in the beginning, but consider people-watching instead. Sit on a park bench or in a chair at the mall and just look around you. Take in the sights and the people interacting with others, and see if you can read their basic body language as a third party looking in.

Once you can master that skill and practice discarding your own personal biases in order to draw distinct conclusions, you can transition into a one-on-one phase, where you are conversing with someone while attempting to analyze them.

Remember, this is a skill, and every skill takes practice.

If you enjoyed this book, please take the time to leave a review on Amazon. I appreciate your honest feedback, and it helps me to continue producing high quality books for people like yourself who are looking for them and the information they hold.

CPSIA information can be obtained
at www.ICGtesting.com
Printed in the USA
LVHW020749190720
661025LV00011B/264